Iranian Diaspora Identities

Iranian Diaspora Identities

Stories and Songs

Ziba Shirazi and Kamran Afary

Hamilton Books

Lanham • Boulder • New York • Toronto • London

Copyright © 2020 by The Rowman & Littlefield Publishing Group, Inc.
An imprint of The Rowman & Littlefield Publishing Group, Inc.
4501 Forbes Boulevard, Suite 200, Lanham, Maryland 20706
Hamilton Books Acquisitions Department (301) 459-3366

6 Tinworth Street, London SE11 5AL, United Kingdom

Library of Congress Control Number: 2020905227
ISBN: 978-0-7618-7170-5 (pbk.)
ISBN: 978-0-7618-7171-2 (electronic)

Contents

Acknowledgments

The authors would like to thank the following persons for the support and help they offered throughout this project. They include translators, poets, editors, our publisher and staff, musicians, photographers, graphic designers, sponsors, academic colleagues and advisers, family, and friends. Ziba would especially like to thank her fans who have always attended her performances. And, a Special thanks to the people who trusted and shared their stories in this book.

Ahou Alagha
Ali Farahani
Ali Makki
Arezoo Koochakan
Aroosha Sarrafi
Ashkon Molaie
Babak Amirebrahimi
Beryl Bellman,
Brooke Bures
Bryant Keith Alexander
Daniel Akhavan
David Olsen
Dori Banki
Esther Klein Buddenhagen
Fariborz Yousefi
Farid Vaghefi
Firouzeh Forouzmand
Frieda Afary
Hadi Khorsandi
Hayedeh Rezghi

Janet Afary
Judith Hamera
Julie E. Kirsch
Mary Kian
Masoud Sepand
Mehdi Fallahi
Mina Abdollahian
Mona Shirazi
Rob DeChaine
Rod Moshtagh
Sadreddin-e Elahi
Sam Brawand
Sanam Salehian
Shahin Espahbodi
Sima Shirazi
Sogol Shirazi
Theresa Larkin
Vandad Espahbodi
Vandad Massahzadeh
William Wilday

A Note on Translations, Monologues, and Stories

The following monologues and stories were originally presented as performances in English and Persian throughout the United States and Canada from interviews conducted from 2009 to 2017. The style of scripting these narratives can best be summed up as, what Bryant Keith Alexander calls "seamlessly moving between auto/ethnography, poetic inquiry, ethnotheatre, and monologue."[1] Some are formatted as a script, others kept as stories in hope that casts of any size, age group, or ethnicity, will perform them and make it their own by either stage reading, added music, enacting characters, or adding props and images. Readers should note that *italics* in the text represent singing by Ziba Shirazi who performed these as one-person shows. Unless otherwise noted, all poetry and lyrics quoted in the monologues and stories are original works by Ziba. Ziba often used an old suitcase as a main prop to signify immigrant memories and journeys. Stage directions have been provided sparingly in the monologues. However, these are less actual stage directions and more an attempt to give the performers a sense of the original interview.

NOTE

1. Bryant Keith Alexander, quoted in Mary E. Weems, *Blackeyed: Plays and Monologues* (Boston: Sense Publishers, 2015), vi.

Introduction

Revolution, War, and the Making of an Iranian Diasporic Literature

The Iranian diaspora is the product of a major social upheaval: a mass revolution followed by the outbreak of a war with Iraq between the years 1978 and 1988.[1] The revolution began with peaceful mass protests and demonstrations in 1977, while industry and agriculture were experiencing major upheavals, and rural populations were fast moving into large cities to occupy homeless encampments. But it was a slanderous article in the *Ettelaat* newspaper on January 7, 1978 against an exiled cleric, Ayatollah Ruhollah Khomeini (d. 1989), living in Iraq at the time, that became the occasion for political demonstrations by young clerical students studying in mosques who were joined by unemployed shantytown dwellers. During the recurrent demonstrations, some were killed, and their martyrdom became a further reason for even larger demonstrations led by public funerals and displays of grief. With this new popular movement, many in the secular left or liberal opposition movements either subsumed their struggles under the banner of the religious right or were simply overshadowed by them.

The exiled Ayatollah Khomeini, who maintained connections with a vast mosque network in Iran and who had a history of uncompromising, fundamentalist opposition to the then current regime, became the titular head of the new upsurge of opposition. He was expelled from Iraq, went to France in autumn of 1978, and was there joined by secular intellectuals and student leaders who also demanded that King Muhammad Reza Shah Pahlavi abdicate. Unable to stem the tide of protests, the Shah left Iran, and Khomeini returned triumphantly on February 1, 1979. Within a few short weeks, the government fell and the army collapsed.

1

The Iranian Revolution, which involved mass participation by the population, was soon branded an "Islamic Republic" in a hastily organized referen-
dum on April 1, but not before women staged massive protests on March 8,
1979 during International Women's Day. In these demonstrations, women
protested the swift reversal of their rights with slogans such as "In the spring
of freedom, there is an absence of freedom." Khomeini's declaration of an
Islamic republic in Iran provoked a period of chaos, as clergy moved swiftly
to eradicate nationalists and left-wing allies to ensure they were excluded
from positions of power. One of the first targets of the clergy's wrath was the
Family Protection Law (FPL), which had provided certain rights and guaran-
tees to women in marriage and divorce—one of the Khomeini's first edicts
was to nullify the FPL. The new regime moved rapidly to disarm secular
neighborhood groups and replace them with mosque-based committees.
These vigilante committees patrolled the streets and enforced Islamic codes
of dress and behavior for women and men. Islamic Revolutionary courts also
moved quickly to arrest and execute scores of army officers, influential political figures, industrialists, and women's rights activists who were branded as
enemies of Islam.

The vigilante groups claimed to protect the country against outside impe-
rialist forces while in reality they worked to intimidate and repress social and
political groups with great brutality. Whenever possible, they tried to erase
obvious signs of Western cultural influence through persecution and violence. These actions convinced tens of thousands that they were no longer
safe in their homeland and had to flee. In November 1979, a group of pro-
Khomeini students seized the U.S. embassy in Tehran and declared this act
an anti-imperialist move. The embassy takeover and the seizure of hostages
soon overshadowed the global solidarity and support that the revolution had
initially garnered in response to the overthrow of the Shah's regime.

While Iranians and the rest of the world were preoccupied with the hostage crisis, a new Islamist constitution was swiftly ratified in November
1980. The new constitution included all the trappings of democratic law,
such as elections for a parliament and president, and term limits for these
positions. But it also created an overarching position of a Supreme Leader for
life who had veto powers over all the elected bodies. The new theocrat,
known as *Vali Faqih*, held his interminable position and had sweeping powers. He controlled the military and was in no way accountable to the legisla-
ture or other branches of government. The new constitution thus wiped away
even the limited democratic rights that the early twentieth-century constitutional movements had established.[2]

In addition to the reign of terror, the outbreak of the Iran-Iraq War (1980-
1988) contributed to mass migration from Iran. In September 1980, Saddam
Hussein's Baathist regime in Iraq invaded Iran's major oil-producing region,
the province of Khuzestan, populated by ethnic Shi'i Arabs of Iran. With the

Iranian military in disarray after the collapse of the Shah's regime, a second armed force was organized to fight the war alongside the regular army. Known as The Revolutionary Guards, this new force was simultaneously fighting a war with Iraq and engaging in suppressing internal dissent in campaigns of repression. With bombings that killed several high-level government figures and changed the atmosphere from revolutionary to war-torn, the Guards engaged in arbitrary arrests in the streets of Iran followed by massive incarceration, widespread torture, and the denial of basic human rights.

By the summer of 1982, Iranian forces were able to push Iraq out of its territory, and the war became a battle for the conquest of Iraq, displaying Khomeini's own imperial ambitions to dominate the region. By this time, internal opposition forces had largely been muzzled, the social movements of ethnic minorities had been crushed, and internal dissenters from within the regime were either killed or forced into exile.

* * *

In "Iran: A Vast Diaspora Abroad and Millions of Refugees at Home," Shirin Hakimzadeh has argued that although the first wave of emigration from Iran began during the 1950s, it was the events both proceeding and immediately following the Islamic Revolution of 1978–1979 that prompted the largest collective emigration.[3] Hakimzadeh claims that over 100,000 Iranians students were studying abroad in the late 1970s. Immediately after the revolution, many of these students decided to remain and were joined by their relatives.

Hakimzadeh divides the population who left in this period into several categories: some were closely associated with the Shah's regime and were able to flee with significant assets. Another group who left Iran immediately during and after the revolution were religious minorities—including Jews, Armenians, Assyrians, and Baha'is who feared religious persecution. This was followed by migration of military and elite families who had connections to the Pahlavi regime. A few months later, a large wave of socialist and liberal intellectuals who feared for their safety and lives followed as well. There were also many young men who refused to serve in the new armed forces who left Iran. Finally, urban middle-class women and their families fled because they could not tolerate living under the new gender-restrictive norms. Hakimzadeh points out that "having a daughter was a decisive factor in a family's decision to flee since the post-revolutionary era forced women to wear the veil, offered [them] decreased educational possibilities, and enforced obedience to male kin."[4]

The exodus soon drained the nation of brainpower as large numbers of academics and professionals left to pursue opportunities in Europe and North

America. Hakimzadeh further notes that many who left in this period, did not consider it to be a permanent move and expected to go back home after a return to normalcy with the demise of the new regime. Very few expected that the new regime would stay in power for decades to come.

PACKING OUR SUITCASES

Whenever we decide to leave our countries of origin to become expatriates, whether one calls us legal or illegal immigrants, whether we are poor or rich, educated or uneducated, single, married, divorced or widowed, there is one thing we expatriates pack in our suitcases—our native culture. We take our culture along with our memories after we separate from our loved ones. We leave almost everything else behind in our home countries in the hope of finding a better home and making a better life for ourselves. Throughout an expatriate's journey from country of origin to country of settlement, the migrant transforms. Moreover, to ensure their survival in the country of settlement, a part of them also dies so that they can be reborn. As the saying goes: Brave ones learn to keep the best of their own culture and mix it with the best of the new culture.[5]

The stories in this collection delve into matters including identity, ethics and morality, relations between parents and children, gender relations, ethnicity, and minority status. The stories explore the cultural shock and difficult process of acculturation, the rites of passage that Iranian immigrants experience, and finally the fractured process of assimilation that is never the same for two individuals. Unlike many other migrants to the United States, Iranians who immigrated to Europe or to the United States in the 1970s through the 1990s were often educated, though many did not speak English. They fled the political persecution of the government of the Islamic Republic in the hopes of achieving greater security, even if it meant a diminution in their standard of living.

Each year a significant number of educated Iranians continue to leave the country. The International Monetary Fund (IMF) has estimated that Iran topped the list of countries who share the unfortunate task of watching their academic elite [leave], with an annual loss of 150,000 to 180,000 specialists, roughly equivalent to a capital loss of $40 billion a year.[6]

Crossing cultures can be a most exciting and rewarding experience, but it can also be a stressful and bewildering one.[7] This has certainly been the case for Iranians. The Islamist revolution of 1979 forced many secular urban and educated Iranians to leave the country. Urban, educated women were particularly hurt as the new government closed daycare centers, demoted the positions of women in the judiciary and in industry, and also reinstated polygamy and easy divorce for men. As a result, a large number of educated middle classes, especially women, left the country. The Revolutionary Guard and its *Basij* morality police on the streets flogged and imprisoned women for violating modesty codes and persecuted religious minorities (Sunni Muslims, Christians, and Jews, and especially Baha'is), as well as many ethnic minorities (Kurds).

These factors also increased emigration rates. Those who fled to the United States faced added political difficulties in their adopted country. Since the hostage crisis of 1979-1980, relations between the United States and Iran have remained tense. Periodically, Iranian migrants and their children have faced harassment and ostracism from the general population in the United States, even though they themselves had fled the persecution of the Islamic Republic. Condescending references to Iranians in the United States, such as "Camel Jockeys" were common in the 1980s.[8] Yet despite such stereotyping, Iranian immigrants managed to excel in their new homelands and have continued to live peacefully, prosperously, and lead productive lives as citizens of their host countries. According to a report by the Migration Policy Institute, a majority of expatriate Iranians hold a bachelor's degree or higher and have gained employment in management and professional fields. A high percentage of expatriate Iranians are also self-employed. In the year 2000, the median income among expatriate Iranian men was $52,333, and, among expatriate Iranian women, the median income was $36,422.[9]

THE IRANIAN DIASPORA IN ACADEMIC STUDIES

Iranian Diaspora Studies as an interdisciplinary academic field is a relatively new one. As research on Iranians' experiences of immigration grew in the 1980s, a new generation of researchers and academics also began to examine the formation of Iranian diaspora cultures and identities. Today, several major universities have Iranian Studies programs and departments with partial funding and endowments provided by Iranian-Americans. In 2016, The Center for Iranian Diaspora Studies at San Francisco State University was founded with a $5 million endowment to research and to teach about the historical and cultural experiences of the global Iranian diaspora. In 2018, an edited volume by Mohsen M. Mobasher titled, *The Iranian Diaspora: Challenges, Negotiations, and Transformations* chronicled the Iranian migrant experiences in eight countries, that is, the United States, five countries in Europe, Australia, and the United Arab Emirates.[10]

Hamid Naficy wrote one of the earliest and most influential academic studies of the Iranian diaspora, *The Making of Exile Cultures.* This work provides a rigorous theoretical framework and intimate details about personal experiences of the exilic community. Specifically, it looks at the ways the Iranian-American popular media in Los Angeles (television, radio, and magazines) redefined and reconstructed a new sense of identity for Iranians during the first decade in exile when they had lost all hope of returning to their native land but had not yet integrated into the new American society. In his introduction, Naficy states,

> The exiles as defined here are not 'native' to either their home or to the host society. They are no longer legally "foreigner" neither are they bona-fide "citizens." They are neither openly, nor secretly, nor dually "marginal." They are not merely "stranger" or "tourists," and they cannot strictly speaking be considered members of an established "ethnic group." Finally, they cannot be entirely characterized as "sojourners," "refugees," or "homeless." Exiles, for the purposes of this work, are none of the above entirely but all of them partially. [11]

Naficy's work is a valuable contribution to the study of how the popular media of Iranians in exile represented and helped construct a new sense of identity out of this experience of liminality.

Ron Kelley and Jonathan Friedlander wrote and edited one of the first ethnographies of the Iranian-American community, titled *Irangeles: Iranians in Los Angeles*.[12] This volume is a collection of essays, interviews, and photographs. It documents the life of Iranian-Americans of Los Angeles as they recreate their old rituals and festivals in a new environment. In some cases, these are stories of formerly persecuted minorities who could not openly celebrate many of these rituals and practices in Iran, so they found new vitality in recreating them in the United States. *Irangeles* captures the diversity of the Iranian immigrant community in Los Angeles. It introduces the reader to a broad range of occupations and income levels, political tendencies, and religious practices within the exilic community. It contains studies of supporters of the former Pahlavi monarchy and even early followers of the Islamic Republic. It also includes vignettes on Muslims, Jews, Zoroastrians, and Baha'is and women of all faiths. The work highlights how new gender roles in the United States were reshaping Iranian women and men and the institution of marriage. Finally, the volume illuminates changes in relations among the Iranian youth and conflicts with their parents.

Zohreh Sullivan's 2001 book *Exiled Memories: Stories of Iranian Diaspora* focuses on narratives and construction of identities through memories.[13] She distinguishes her work from empirical sociological studies of Iranians in America and argues that the reconstruction of memory and identity is an important part of how Iranians in the United States experience themselves. Sullivan's work highlights issues of difference, relationality, and local knowledge that shape a discourse about the transitions experienced as Iranians moved from one culture to another after the revolution.

Babak Elahi and Persis Karim, devoted a special issue of *Comparative Studies of South Asia, Africa and the Middle East* to the Iranian Diaspora.[14]

The authors argue that those Iranians who left Iran during 1979-1988 manifest a unique experience that merits the title of "Iranian diaspora." They point out that there is a critical tension between the use of the term diaspora and exile or immigration, because the former engenders its own unique questions. They have also sought to extend this new study to Iranians living outside of North America to include those living in Asia or Australia. Karim's work on the Iranian diaspora also includes a focus on the experience of women as in her *Let Me Tell You Where I've Been: New Writing by Women of the Iranian Diaspora*.[15]

Another essay argues for more autobiographical and narrative studies. In her essay, "Autobiography and Authority in the Writings of the Iranian Diaspora," Amy Motlagh suggests that the proliferation of popular memoirs by Iranian-American women is a way in which the Iranian diaspora community produces (and reproduces) itself while examining and expanding the limits of authenticity and authority.[16]

Likewise, Amy Malek, in her "Public Performances of Identity Negotiation in the Iranian Diaspora: The New York Persian Day Parade," documents how in the last decade, in the face of hostility by Americans towards Middle Eastern immigrants, Iranian-Americans have asserted their cultural and ethnic identity on streets and fairgrounds holding ethnic parades and festivals, just as Irish, German, and Puerto Rican American communities did before them.[17]

Iranian diaspora studies have embraced issues of gender and sexuality both as identity and as practice. In her 2012 "Diasporic Masculinities," Fataneh Farahani reflects on her ethnographic fieldwork. In her comparative study she examines the lives of Iranian men as they left Iran, arrived, and settled in Sydney, Stockholm, and London.[18] Farahani develops a framework to examine the formation and continual negotiation of masculinity among Iranian men, a negotiation that involves not only re-examining gender relations but other issues such as religion, race, age, class, the relationship between individual and community, and politics. Shadee Abdi and Bobbi Van Gilder have focused on cultural invisibility of Iranian-American queer women. In their study, they explore the narratives of twelve first-generation, queer, Iranian-American women to understand how Iranian cultural, familial, and relational discourses influence feelings of "belonging," and how they cope with the challenges of being both LGBTQ and Iranian-American.[19] They further expand this work by exploring modes of the management of sexual identities by Iranian-American queer women.

IRANIAN DIASPORA IN POPULAR LITERATURE

Memoirs primarily written by Iranian-American women comprise a second genre of work on Iranian-Americans. Some of these women grew up in Iran and settled in the United States. Others came to the United States as children and then returned to live in Iran for several years. They write about memories of growing up in Iran or in Iranian households in the United States. An author of one of these memoirs is Azadeh Moaveni. She begins with her recollections of growing up in California, feeling conflicted about her identity. She ends up moving back to Iran as a journalist. Moaveni describes her experiences as living in two worlds: "At home in California, I was the daughter of an Iranian exile community, serving tea, clinging to tradition, and dreaming of Tehran. Outside, I was a California girl who practiced yoga and listened to Madonna."[20]

Others, like Roya Hakakian, wrote about growing up in a Jewish family in Iran and then moving abroad.[21] Although she wrote it twenty years after she emigrated from Iran, it is entirely about her Iranian experience. She especially explores the contradictions within Iranian minority communities and how they negotiated interethnic relations.

Persepolis, by Marjane Satrapi, is a graphic novel (and later film) and a global phenomenon.[22] Satrapi adopts the format of *Maus*, a graphic novel that depicts the experience of Art Spiegleman's father, a Holocaust survivor from Poland.[23] Satrapi blends a detailed narrative about Iran's 1979 Revolution with an intimate portrayal of the ramifications of that event for herself and her family. She provides a general history and also a particular representation of the life of an Iranian woman who is forced to leave Iran at a young age. She shows not only the persecution of Iranians and their mistreatment at the hands of the morality police, but also the trials she suffered in Europe as she faced racism and sexism, alienation, homelessness, and subsequent depression and mental health issues.

Satrapi describes her life in Austria with a group of nuns at a religious school and a family she stayed with. Her account includes a strong critique of the nihilistic avant-garde youth of Europe. As a young woman who had just experienced a revolution, a war, exile, and murder, she finds the nihilistic attitude of counter-culture youth and their total disregard for social reality nauseating. As the world around her starts disintegrating, she abandons school and becomes homeless for a while before returning to Iran.

Foojan Zeine and Mahnaz Attarha published another remarkable, and as yet not translated, novel in Los Angeles called *Mā* (We) in 2014.[24] This is a collaborative work that depicts email conversations between a 50-year-old woman and her therapist. The woman delves deeply into her inner voices, characters that reveal stories of gender persecution and sexism for generations of Iranian women. This process of therapeutic narrative dialogue is carried out in the context of the Iranian diaspora experience.

Yet another notable memoir is *Reading Lolita in Tehran* by Azar Nafisi. This is another example of Iranian diaspora literature that has gained global recognition. Nafisi's work is a powerful exploration of the East-West relationship, and the way in which literature from one continent can resonate with another over than a century later. Nafisi chronicles her study group that was composed of young Iranian women in Tehran in the 1980s. She describes how these sessions became a way for the participants to intertwine their own life stories with those in the works they were reading.[25]

Reading Lolita in Tehran explores the liberating power of literature in the face of tyranny. Nafisi shows how Anglo-Saxon literature from the late eighteenth to the first half of the twentieth century, which may no longer resonate with western audiences, can be meaningful to young Iranian women. Jane Austen's famous opening line in *Pride and Prejudice* that "It is a truth universally acknowledged, that a single man in possession of a good fortune, must be in want of a wife,"[26] speaks to the experiences of Iranian women in the 1980s.

IRANIAN DIASPORA IN PERFORMANCES

Rogers Brubaker argues that the rapid expansion of diaspora as a conceptual mode of study, while having the advantage of going beyond a nationalist framework, carries the assumption that a community is another bounded group with a predetermined destiny of waking up to a fated true identity.[27] He argues that diaspora, instead, is a category in the process of constant remaking. Theater productions created in the diaspora by Iranian-Americans provide another window into this ongoing process as artists chronicle the process by which a creative mode of practicing one's own identity formation takes place.

Writing about Iranian theater productions in Toronto, Marjan Moosavi explains that theater artists have created a viable community by facing and persevering through challenges from a harsh material reality, existential fears, language barriers, and the complications of navigating grant application processes.[28] By getting involved in cultural and community activism, theatre producers, performers, and playwrights are able to engage in self-reflection and in healing.

Staging Iranian diaspora identities in the dramas of everyday life, Tara Grammy's multi-national perspective is enacted in *Mahmoud* an irreverent and hilarious one-woman show about an aging Iranian engineer-cum-taxi driver, a fabulously gay Spaniard, and a young Iranian-Canadian girl, all trying to get through the day-to-day grind in a busy metropolitan city.[29]

Delving into modern Iranian literature and poetry for a greater diasporic audience, Sussan Deyhim's *The House is Black* was celebrated as a major theatrical event in Los Angeles in 2013.[30] The play is inspired by the writings and filmmaking of Forough Farrokhzad, an influential feminist poet whose work is still relevant for women today, despite her untimely passing at the age of 32 years in the 1960s. Deyhim creates a series of non-linear poetic tableaux of some of the most intimate and provocative writings by Forough.

Shabnam Tolouei's *Autumn Dance* is a play that follows three tormented Iranian women experiencing exile, even while two of them are living in their own country. Bita, a journalist, and Mojdeh, a prostitute, are both imprisoned in Iran's infamous Evin prison. A third woman, Yekta, lives in exile in Paris. The simple elegance of the play allows the audience to be transported from Tehran to Paris to uncover the connection between these three women. Tolouei, an award-winning actress, playwright, and director, plays all three roles.[31]

Born in Tehran in a Baha'i family, Tolouei was forced into exile because of the persecution of Baha'i minorities in Iran. She currently lives and works in France. Tolouei also directed the film, *Dust, Flower, Flame* (2016), which shows the similarities between women's lives in Iran today and the life of the nineteenth-century poet and theologian, revolutionary and rebellious figure of the Baha'i faith, Tahereh Qorrat al-Ayn. Tolouei writes, "The status of women in Iran is unfortunately the same as it was 170 years ago when Qurratolein paid a price for her freedom of opinion."[32]

The celebrated Iranian-American visual artist and film director, Shirin Neshat, whose artwork centers on contrasts and the differences between Islam and the West as well as and femininity and masculinity, has also produced films that inform Iranian diasporic identities.[33] In both her full feature films, *Looking for Oum Kulthum* (2017) and *Women Without Men* (2009), Neshat narrates the recurring narratives of central characters, Middle Eastern women who choose to pursue a talent or a professional career and face life in male-dominated societies where they experience similar predicaments.[34]

A new generation of Iranian-American comics is also navigating life events and responding to a surge of anti-Muslim pressures in the U.S through literature. A good representative of this genre is Zahra Noorbakhsh's *All Atheists Are Muslim*. Her work was dubbed by the *New Yorker* magazine a highlight of the New York International Fringe Festival. She wrote an opinion piece in the *New York Times* in which her response to unremitting expectations that she present herself as a Muslim comedian who is "just like you" was, "I'm finally asserting my right to be 'just like' any other comedian and, more important, just like myself."[35]

Another mainstream Iranian-American comic who is a regular guest on late-night television shows and on NPR is Maz Jobrani. His *Axis of Evil Comedy Tour* (2005) was an attempt at shaping the American public opinion about people of the Middle East and an ironic take on George W. Bush's 2002 designation of Iran, Iraq, and North Korea as the axis of evil. Film critic Leah Pickett writes that Jobrani's character, Jimmy Vestvood, is a "jab at American prejudices toward the Middle East."[36] The Jimmy Vestvood character comes to the United States by winning a green-card lottery and dreams of becoming an American cop while working as a security guard at a Persian grocery store. Enthusiastically waving an American flag while smoking, he accidentally sets the flag on fire! Caught on video, he is mistakenly identified by "Kox News" as a jihadist. With a touch of Borat, this is a film about an inept hero and an unending series of gags.

In 2011, in the aftermath of the 2009 Green Movement uprising, there was a surge of both new exiles who entered the United States and Europe and new productions in the United States that aimed at supporting democratic tendencies in Iran. *Iranian Voices*, a collaborative project led by the Swedish National Theatre, created a series of radio documentaries from true stories with the goal of making voices of the Iranian Diaspora accessible to a global community.

A number of directors have tried to create works of art that are a fusion of multiple cultures beyond only Iranian and American cultures. A great example of fusion is Torange Yeghiazarian's *Isfahan Blues*. The play is based on the Duke Ellington Orchestra's 1963 tour to Iran. Yeghiazarian imagines an unlikely friendship between the jazz musician and an Iranian actress as they travel together to Isfahan. Yeghiazarian is a founder of the Golden Thread theater company in the San Francisco Bay Area, and she defines her company's mission as "exposing non-Middle Eastern audiences to the authentic voice and alternative perspective of the region, while serving Middle Eastern audiences who rarely encounter meaningful reflections of their own culture in the performing arts."[37]

The appearance of these works in the English language in the United States, and the enthusiastic responses they have received suggest that the literature on the Iranian Diaspora is not just aimed at Iranian or Iranian-American society but has been embraced by many in the world. The difference between the present work and the existing literature discussed above is that this is the first attempt to gather in print the actual stories of the Iranian diaspora population, those who left during and soon after the Iranian Revolution, to perform them before live audiences, and to analyze them in the context of theories of communication.

METHODOLOGY, RESEARCH QUESTIONS, AND PURPOSE

Our study is, in part, performance ethnography that relies on both participant observation and on the gathering of data on cultural formations. Ziba Shirazi gathered stories and performed them in front of live audiences of Iranians in the diaspora as well as non-Iranians. She named the project *Story & Song* and took the first performance on stage in Los Angeles in the fall of 2009. Since then, she has given more than sixty performances in the United States and Canada, and more than 19,000 people have seen them. Based on interactions and observations with fans and followers through email and personal contact, Shirazi estimates that about 60% of her followers are female, 95% have a college education, and their average age is 45 years. Shirazi's childhood dream of playing the leading role came true in 2009 when she took the first performance of *Story & Song* on stage. The performance involved a mix of music, poetry, imagery, and movement.

Anna Deavere-Smith inspired many aspects of these stories, including the retelling and the analysis. Her performances capture a complex social reality and stage it with multiple characters. She created a new form of theatre by performing each story as an outsider with multiple points of view using minimum props: "a blend of theatrical art, social commentary, journalism, and intimate reverie."[38]

In our discussions on how to gather the stories, stage them, and finally publish them in this volume, we were also influenced by performance studies scholars including Victor Turner and Dwight Conquergood, as well as by cultural theorist John Berry.

Like Turner, in choosing qualitative narrative we were able to empathize with each participant's pains, sorrows, and joys of accomplishments. In analyzing these stories, we also demonstrate how rhetorical criticism and communication theory can help make sense of these journeys. We are motivated by a narrative model of rhetoric that pays close attention to how stories are constructed. Turner's concept of liminality and his theory of social drama with its four stages of development—breach, crisis, redressive performances, and schism or reintegration—were of key importance to our work.[39] These stages of development help researchers theorize the stories they gather during the process of fieldwork.

Dwight Conquergood's writings on performance ethnography was an important inspiration for our work.[40] Afary was a student of Conquergood's, and as Shirazi began to gather data in the field, they discussed the implications of Conquergood's work for the stories Shirazi was collecting. Conquergood sees the body as the center of expression, knowledge, mind and soul, and a tool for experiencing and sharing stories. He believes in dialogue and the act of listening at the time of research. One of Conquergood's most famous contributions is the concept of a "dialogical performance" between researcher and subject of study. He warns against pitfalls in ethnography that range from selfishness and cynicism to superficiality and sensationalism.

Instead, Conquergood calls for a genuine conversation and dialogue in his famous "moral mapping" and "ethics of representation."[41] Shirazi and Afary attempted to emulate Conquergood's concept of "moral mapping," in their relationship to the diasporic Iranian community. Moral mapping suggests an ethical dialogical approach to ethnography during fieldwork, one that involves both listening closely and contributing back to the process that guides one's research and performances.

To encourage participants to share their stories, it helped that Shirazi wrote and performed her own story first and talked about her struggles and hardships along with her mistakes and naïve choices in life and the lessons learned, to precisely develop an empathic relationship with her audience. She was not there to judge them and point out their mistakes. She had experienced much of what they had experienced, comprehended what they had gone through, and realized how much courage it took to survive and even flourish afterwards.

Conquergood had also made a further contribution to various theories of performance. An old school of thought, raised first by Aristotle, assumed that performances were mimesis, simply an imitation of experience, but not real. Mimesis suggests that performances are fake and manipulative and Aristotle's definition gave rise to an anti-theatrical prejudice. Victor Turner argued that performances were more than just imitations. They were in fact poiesis, or what creates culture when we embody different identities in our cultural performances. Conquergood argued that performances could be kinesis. Performances were more than poiesis, in that they could actively intervene in "breaking and remaking" culture. [42]

A performance, when done well, has the ability to invoke something new in us. Shirazi's hope in her performances and in coauthoring this book has been that it helps make her performances a form of kinesis for the diasporic Iranian community.

Finally, we found John Berry's analysis of the psychology of ethnic groups in the United States—especially his account of how each individual has different responses to acculturation—very useful. Berry points out that migrants might go through any of the following stages or a combination of them: (1) assimilation, when an individual wishes to identify with the other culture rather than his/her own; (2) separation, when an individual holds on to the culture of origin and avoids learning the new culture; (3) marginalization, when the individual does not involve much with either culture; neither with the culture of origin nor any other culture; and (4) integration, when the individual maintains the culture of origin while participating in the other culture. [43] Berry's model provides an important framework for understanding and analyzing the Iranian diasporic experience and the stories in this volume.

PRELIMINARY RESEARCH QUESTIONS

This work began by asking several preliminary research questions about Iranian immigration abroad. These questions were influenced by the preceding discussion of theories of communication and methods of ethnography. The themes of the research included the following:

1. How did the first generation of Iranian immigrants, those who left during or immediately after the 1979 Revolution, negotiate the difficult circumstances they faced?
2. What were the negative and positive aspects of the experience of Iranian migration that led to personal growth and transformation for them?
3. What were some of the specific features of intercultural communication that those in the Iranian diaspora experienced? How can we gain a better understanding of Iranian immigrants' lived experiences?
4. What were some of the lessons that these Iranian-Americans drew from these experiences?
5. Is there a correlation between age, level of education, gender, and date of entry of diasporic Iranians and their response to possible forms of acculturation, as defined by John Berry?

These questions and the theories that motivated them guided us in establishing a link between storytelling, culture, performance, oral history, political commentary, and communication. We have, therefore, analyzed the stories in the context of communication studies and critical and performance ethnography.

PURPOSE OF THE STUDY

In *Remembering: Oral History Performance*, Della Pollock argues that "a story is not a story until it is told; it is not told until it is heard, once it is heard, it changes . . . a story is not a story until it changes."[44] Sharing personal life stories and having them publicly performed in front of audiences has never been widely practiced by Iranian artists, especially by women. There is a tradition of popular storytelling in Persian literature called *naqqāli*, epic storytelling. In *naqqāli*, the narrator tells stories through reciting poetry from the *Shahnameh* (Book of Kings), written by Ferdowsi (d. 1020) a millennium ago. These storytelling sessions are mostly staged at old coffeehouses, which until recently were segregated and included only male patrons and performers.

However, after the Islamic Revolution, a few female artists broke the taboo, and after years of struggle, succeeded to learn the techniques of *naqqāli* and take it onto the stage abroad.[45] By performing Iranian immigrants' stories, Shirazi has reproduced a form of *naqqāli* for our time and place. Through these stories we come to develop a deeper understanding of Iranians, those living in Iran or abroad and move beyond Western stereotypes of the community. In this way, we hope the stories would bring Iranian and non-Iranians closer to one another. Performance, ethnography, culture, and storytelling.

Storytelling is a cooperation and collaboration between the teller and the recipients. Through storytelling we define who we are and what our beliefs are, we transmit our values, ideals and our dreams. In this way "performances are constitutive of culture, not something added to the culture."[46] In other words, cultural performances constitute social experience; they are not additive tools to understand culture. By performing storytelling, Shirazi portrays Iranians' culture, as well as their beliefs, values, and perceptions of obstacles and problems as they, as individuals, move through unfamiliar settings.

PROCESS: INTERVIEWS, EDITING, POETRY, AND MUSIC

The process started with Shirazi gathering data through in-depth interviews and conversations with the participants in an attempt to uncover deeper meaning and understanding of how migration had affected them socially, culturally, and personally.

Shirazi made initial personal contact with the volunteer participants by calling them on the phone or by emailing. She explained the process and the time needed (a minimum of three hours). Before starting the face-to-face interviews, she showed them her digital voice recording device and told them that their voice would be recorded and erased after transcription. She started the interviews by asking an open-ended question: When and why did you leave Iran?

Most participants started by going back to the time prior to the 1979 Islamic Revolution, talking about their social and political status at the time, and then moved forward. While answering the above two questions, the interviewee covers the following subjects:

1. How did you leave Iran? Did you leave legally—from the airport, by land—or illegally—fleeing or using a smuggler.
2. Where was your first landing/arriving?
3. What was your level of education?
4. Did you speak the language of the host country?

5. What kind of visa did you have when you entered your host country?
6. Have you acquired citizenship? How did you get your citizenship?
7. What was your job and social class in Iran?
8. What was your first job in your host country?
9. What is your best memory?
10. What is your worst memory?
11. Can you share a memory about language barriers?
12. Have you or would you ever go back to Iran for a visit?
13. Would you consider living in Iran, if the situation drastically improves?

Many times, Shirazi became a participant-observer by sharing her own personal stories, crying or laughing with them, trying to comfort them or praise them for their courage, bravery, patience, and strength. Sometimes she interacted in order to clarify something, but usually the more they shared, the more detail-oriented the interview became. Often these stories emotionally affected Shirazi, especially at the time of rehearsal. In preparing for the performances, the more Shirazi rehearsed and became in-tune with her participants' stories, the more she felt she understood their pains, their sorrows, and their joys.

The second step was to transcribe the recordings, word-for-word, in order to come close to the emotion and the language used by the participants. Transcribing usually took eight hours per interview, and the end result was approximately fifty to fifty-five pages. Shirazi took special care to transcribe every recording word-for-word and also to capture the tone and the emotional texture as best as she could. She paid attention to what was important to them, the emotion in their voice, and the wording they used.

The third step was editing the Persian text of the interviews, which was the most time consuming. Here, Shirazi decided what to keep and what to eliminate since it was important to limit the performance to a fixed time to keep the audience interested while staying true to the story.

The final step was for the performances to incorporate cultural memory and to add a sense of identity by using music and poetry. Although there are a few poems from famous Iranian poets in these performances, Shirazi typically composed original poems for each story to convey the texture of the feelings in that particular story. Poetry serves to amplify the sorrow, pain, happiness, and exaltation; to highlight what seems to be the closure of one chapter and the opening of another in a person's life story. Poetry is a major part of *Story & Song* as it connects to a foundational aspect of Iranian culture. As Dr. H. Elahi Ghomshei writes in *The Rose and the Nightingale*, "Poetry in Persian culture is not simply an art: rather it's the very image of life, terrestrial and celestial; the perennial philosophy, the holy scripture, the minstrel, the music and the song, the feast and revelry, the garden, the rose and the nightingale, and a detailed agenda for daily life."[47] While participants express their feeling about an experience, Shirazi, as a storyteller, honors their experiences, intensifying the meanings by adding poetry.

The English translations are a collaborative process of both authors. There are many words that are not easily translatable, words that link to one's culture, memory, and background, and we spent a great deal of time trying to come up with equivalents that conveyed a similar sense in the English language.

On stage, Shirazi sings and plays the guitar. Sometimes, she hires other professional musicians to accompany her. Shirazi's fame within the Iranian community as a singer is perhaps a main draw for the audiences of *Story & Song* who come expecting a concert rather than a collection stories. In fact, storytelling in this modern form is totally new to them.

Performing these stories to the very individuals who shared them with Shirazi in the first place proved to be a healing and therapeutic experience for them. It gave these individuals an opportunity to be heard and to see their lives performed on stage from another perspective.

Throughout this period of developing a research topic, selecting methodology, conducting ethnographic fieldwork, and staging performances, Shirazi and Afary consulted regularly to weave together concepts of intercultural and interpersonal communication theory and a performance ethnography approach. Upon the completion of this phase, Shirazi and Afary worked together to write up the study and prepare the present volume.

We hope this study is useful for future Iranian immigrants as well as for students, scholars, and researchers of immigration and Diaspora Studies. We also believe that educators, psychologists, professionals in the field of immigration may benefit from the trajectory of this work and the stories within. The experiences, issues, and problems that Iranian immigrants faced at the turn of the twenty-first century, while adapting to a new life in the United States, have provided many lessons for the new populations of immigrants.

NOTES

1. See Mohsen M. Milani, "The Iranian Islamic Revolution (1979)," in *Encyclopedia of Political Revolutions*, ed. Jack Goldstone (London: Fitzroy Dearborn, 1998; repr. New York: Routledge, 2015), 248; and *Janet* Afary, "Iranian Revolution [1978–1979]," in *Encyclopædia Britannica*. Encyclopædia Britannica, https://www.britannica.com/event/Iranian-Revolution (accessed September 20, 2017); as well as the authors' personal recollections. Kamran Afary was a news reporter and documentary producer during the period 1979 to 1998 when he covered the events of Iran for KPFK Radio, a Pacifica station in Los Angeles.

2. On the history of that earlier revolution, see Janet Afary, *The Iranian Constitutional Revolution, 1906–1911: Grassroots Democracy, Social Democracy, and the Origins of Feminism* (New York: Columbia University Press, 1996).

3. Shirin Hakimzadeh, "Iran: A Vast Diaspora Abroad and Millions of Refugees at Home," *Migration Information Source* 4 (2006), https://www.migrationpolicy.org/article/iran-vast-di-aspora-abroad-and-millions-refugees-home (accessed September 30, 2019).

4. Hakimzadeh, "Iran."

5. Here we use the term *culture* in the sense introduced by Raymond Williams as "ordinary, the common meanings and directions of a society. These meanings are learned, made, and remade by individuals." Elizabeth Bell, *Theories of Performance* (Thousand Oaks, CA: SAGE Publications, 2008), 116. See also Williams. *The Long Revolution* (Ontario: Broadview Press, 1961).

6. International Monetary Fun (IMF), quoted in Frances Harrison, "Huge Cost of Iranian Brain Drain," *BBC News* (Middle East), January 08, 2007, http://news.bbc.co.uk/2/hi/middle_east/6240287.stm (accessed September 30, 2019).

7. Colleen A. Ward, Stephen Bochner, and Adrian Furnham, *The Psychology of Culture Shock*, 2nd ed. (Philadelphia: Taylor & Francis, 2001).

8. Thomas R. Haggard, with Tracey C. Green and Leigh Nason, *Understanding Employment Discrimination*, 2nd ed. (Newark, NJ: LexisNexis Mathew Bender, 2008).

9. Shirin Hakimzadeh and David Dixon, "Spotlight on the Iranian Foreign Born," Migration Policy Institute, 2006, https://www.migrationpolicy.org/article/spotlight-iranian-foreign-born (accessed October 1, 2019).

10. Mohsen Mostafavi Mobasher, *The Iranian Diaspora: Challenges, Negotiations, and Transformations* (Austin: University of Texas Press, 2018).

11. Hamid Naficy, *The Making of Exile Cultures: Iranian Television in Los Angeles* (Minneapolis: University of Minnesota Press, 1993), 16.

12. *Irangeles: Iranians in Los Angeles*, ed. Ron Kelley and Jonathan Friedlander (Berkeley: University of California Press, 1993).

13. Zohreh T. Sullivan, *Exiled Memories: Stories of Iranian Diaspora* (Philadelphia: Temple University Press, 2001).

14. Babak Elahi and Persis M. Karim, "Introduction: Iranian Diaspora," *Comparative Studies of South Asia, Africa and the Middle East* 31, no. 2 (2011): 381–87, https://doi.org/10.1080/00210862.2012.740896.

15. *Let Me Tell You Where I've Been: New Writing by Women of the Iranian Diaspora*, ed. Persis M. Karim (Fayetteville: University of Arkansas Press, 2006).

16. Amy Motlagh, "Autobiography and Authority in the Writings of the Iranian Diaspora," *Comparative Studies of South Asia, Africa and the Middle East* 31, no. 2 (2011): 411–24, https://doi.org/10.1215/1089201X-1264325.

17. Amy Malek, "Public Performances of Identity Negotiation in the Iranian Diaspora: The New York Persian Day Parade," *Comparative Studies of South Asia, Africa and the Middle East* 31, no. 2 (2011): 388–410, https://doi.org/10.1215/1089201X-1264316.

18. Fataneh Farahani, "Diasporic Masculinities," *Nordic Journal of Migration Research* 2, no. 2 (2012): 159–66, https://doi.org/10.2478/v10202-011-0038-5.

19. Shadee Abdi and Bobbi Van Gilder, "Cultural (In)visibility and Identity Dissonance: Queer Iranian-American Women and Their Negotiation of Existence," *Journal of International and Intercultural Communication*. 9, no. 1 (2016): 69–86, https://doi.org/10.1080/1751305 7.2016.1120850."

20. Azadeh Moaveni, *Lipstick Jihad: A Memoir of Growing Up Iranian in America and American in Iran* (New York: Public Affairs, 2005), 12.

21. Roya Hakakian, *Journey from the Land of No* (New York: Crown, 2004).

22. Marjane Satrapi, *Persepolis: The Story of a Childhood* (New York: Pantheon, 2003).

23. See Art Spiegelman, *Maus : A Survivor's Tale* (New York: Pantheon, 1991).

24. Foojan Zeine and Mahnaz Attarha, *Mā* (Persian Edition) (Bloomington, IN: XLIBIRS, 2014).

25. Azar Nafisi, *Reading Lolita in Tehran: A Memoir in Books* (New York: Random House, 2003).

26. Jane Austen, *Pride and Prejudice* (New York: Modern Library, 1995), 3.

27. Rogers Brubaker, "The 'Diaspora' Diaspora" *Ethnic and Racial Studies* 28, no. 1 (2006): 1–19, https://doi.org/10.1080/0141987042000289997.

28. Marjan Moosavi, "Acclimatization: Feminist Iranian Theatre Acclimatizes to Diaspora," *Theatre Times*, June 9, 2018, https://thetheatretimes.com/acclimatization-feminist-iranian-theatre-acclimatizes-diaspora/ (accessed September 30, 2019).

29. Tara Grammy and Tom Arthur Davis, *Mahmoud* (Toronto: Playwrights Canada Press, 2015).

30. See Sussan Deyhim, *The House is Black*, Vimeo video, 02:25, posted by "CAP UCLA," 2014, https://vimeo.com/109868198.

31. See trailer, Shabnam Tolouei, *"Autumn Dance*, by Shabnam Tolouei," YouTube video, 00:52, Posted by Stanford Iranian Studies Program. July 18, 2017, https://www.youtube.com/watch?v=DgjM5s24zMM.

32. Shabnam Tolouei, "Iran's First Feminist Qorrat al-Ayn is Brought Back to Life in New Movie," interview with Katayhoon Halajan, *Kayhan Life*, November 16, 2016, https://kayhanlife.com/culture/film/irans-first-feminist-qorrat-al-ayn-brought-back-life-new-movie/ (accessed September 30, 2019).

33. Shirin Neshat, Ahmad Diba, and Shirin Neshat, *Looking for Oum Kulthum*, directed by Shirin Neshat and Shoja Azari (Geneva: Agora Films, 2017).

34. Shirin Neshat and Shoja Azari, *Women Without Men*, DVD, directed by Shirin Neshat and Shoja Azari (New York: IndiPix, 2009).

35. Zahra Noorbakhsh, "It's Not This Muslim Comedian's Job to Open Your Mind," *New York Times*, May 6, 2017, https://www.nytimes.com/2017/05/06/opinion/sunday/its-not-this-muslim-comedians-job-to-open-your-mind.html (accessed September 30, 2019).

36. Leah Pickett, review of "Jimmy Vestvod: *Amerikan Hero*," 2016, *Chicago Reader*, https://www.chicagoreader.com/chicago/jimmy-vestvood-amerikan-hero/Film?oid=23603696 (accessed September 30, 2019).

37. Torange Yeghiazarian, "About Golden Thread Productions," *Golden Thread*. https://www.goldenthread.org/about/ (last accessed 2018); https://goldenthread.org/about/ (accessed September 30, 2019). See also Isfahan Blues, "About Golden Thread Productions," *Golden Thread*, https://www.goldenthread.org/2015-season/isfahan-blues/ (last accessed 2018), https://goldenthread.org/about/ (accessed September 30, 2019).

38. MacArthur Foundation, "Anna Deavere Smith," *MacArthur Foundation*, July 1, 1996, last updated January 1, 2005, https://www.macfound.org/fellows/544/ (accessed September 30, 2019).

39. Victor Turner, "Liminality and Communitas," in *The Performance Studies Reader*, 2nd ed., ed. Henry Bial (New York: Routledge, 2007), 89–97.

40. See Dwight Conquergood, "Performance Studies: Interventions and Radical Research," in *The Performance Studies Reader*, 2nd ed., ed. Henry Bial (New York: Routledge, 2007), 369–80.

41. Dwight Conquergood, "Performing as a Moral Act: Ethical Dimensions of the Ethnography of Performance," *Literature in Performance* 5, no. 2 (1985): 1–13, https://doi.org/10.1080/10462938509391578.

42. Dwight Conquergood, "Of Caravans and Carnivals: Performance Studies in Motion," *TDR* (MIT Press) 39, no. 4 (1995): 138, https://www.jstor.org/stable/1146488.

43. John W. Berry, "Acculturation: Living Successfully in Two Cultures," *International Journal of Intercultural Relations* 29, no. 6 (2005): 697–712, https://doi.org/10.1016/j.ijintrel.2005.07.013.

44. *Remembering: Oral History Performance*, ed. Della Pollock (New York and Basingstoke, UK: Palgrave Macmillan, 2005), 81.

45. For the work of the most celebrated female *naqqāl* Gordafarid, currently residing in Los Angeles, see a video of her performance at LACMA. "Gordafarid Presents the Story of Gordafarid and Sohrab // Performances," Vimeo video, 8:42, posted by "LACMA," May 2, 2018, https://vimeo.com/268865001.

46. Carolon Ellis, *Final Negotiations: A Story of Love, Loss, and Chronic Illness* (Philadelphia, PA: Temple University Press, 1995), 116.

47. Hossein Elahi Ghomshei, "The Rose and the Nightingale: The Role of Poetry in Persian Culture," *SGI Quarterly* 51 (2007): 6, https://www.sgi.org/content/files/resources/sgi-quarterly-magazine/0801_51.pdf. (last accessed May 16, 2015).

Monologues

One

My Rite of Passage and Unexpected Fate

Ziba Shirazi

(Setting: An old suitcase with a shawl over it in the middle of stage. A high stool, guitar on a stand. Ziba sings.)

> *I missed the good old days*
> *Though I've changed in many ways.*
> *I was raised to be praised*
> *Till this day I am amazed*
> *I walked a bumpy road and paved it*
> *I took a chance, and I made it.* [1]

It was not supposed to end like this. (Demanding voice)
Not at all!
I wasn't supposed to worry about bread on my table!
I wasn't supposed to worry about my next month's rent!
I wasn't supposed to live from paycheck to paycheck!
I never thought checking my mailbox would become such a horrifying experience.
My sister is right to say, "The only man who always finds his way into our house is 'Bill'!"
Let me tell you what I expected my life to be like (Soft voice)
Although the memory will only tear at my heart, (Sarcastically sad)
And maybe yours, too, ladies.
I expected to find a man, (Soft voice)
A gentleman,
An educated, neat rich man,
But most of all, a man in love with me:

23

So in love with me that he would be ready to work from dawn to dusk and
     come home with his arms full of gifts.
His arms so full that he would have to open the door with his foot!
I was supposed to stay home and care for the children and play the good
     wife to Mr. So and So.[2]
We would reach an understanding that every now and then we would
     have a guest, and I would rely on my feminine wisdom to know for
     whom to open the door and whom to keep out of our lives.[3]
Despite all the things that were not supposed to happen,
Something was bound to happen that I had no clue about.
There was supposed to be a REVOLUTION!

> *A holy man came to town*
> *He overthrew the crown*
> *He forbade happiness and joy*
> *He didn't care that he destroyed*

Yes, the revolution came and took us all by surprise
It was mind-blowingly shocking.
In fact, the revolution rushed us to our unknown fates.
It's true that we the people spoke the same language,
But the rulers views did not match the spirit of many of us
We were forced into a life of deception.
We were forced to live two separate lives:
One hidden in our homes, (Low voice)
The other out in public.
Our life inside was close to who we were.
We held secret parties, (With a half-smile)
We listened to our music
We danced our dances
We laughed. (Pause)
In time, we even became addicted to the thrill of our underground joy.
     (Pause)
Simultaneously, we created a fake persona out in the street,
Perfectly in harmony with strict Islamic rules; to face the Islamic author-
     ities.
It was our survival strategy.
This went on for what seemed like forever, until many of us could no
     longer live with two selves and a double consciousness. (Pause)
So, we immigrated to the West
In hopes of a better life,
One truer to our nature
Despite the unbearable pain of separation from loved ones

> *Farewell my love, farewell*

It's time to leave: I'm compelled
I am migrating like a sparrow
Leaving behind all my sorrow [4]

The only thing in my head in those days was to leave the land that had become unlivable.
I yearned for freedom;
I thought if I left Iran, life would be heaven.
I'd go wherever I wanted
Whenever I wanted.
I'd do whatever I wanted.
I'd wear whatever my heart desired.
I'd lie by a pool under the naked sun, and let my body absorb every atom
I had thought of everything BUT how to earn a living! (Looking incredulously)
I thought it wouldn't make any difference
One way or another.
The same dreamboat who was to be my husband in Iran, working from dawn to dusk
Was destined to find me in America! (Assured voice)
It would be the same perfect gentleman
Only maybe with blond hair and blue eyes
What difference does it make?
It's the spirit that counts! (Smiling)
Actually, you know what?
My best friend married an American
A blond American to boot!
And her mother kept telling me:

"Ziba dear, get yourself an American husband and you'll be set for life"

The old woman was worried
She knew I was once married to an Iranian; she thought maybe an American husband would turn my life around!
Years later it finally dawned on me that I should not rely on a man, American or Iranian, to set me up for life. (Three-second pause)
Did any of you ever hear this story? (Half smile)
Two sisters went to the American consulate in the early years of the revolution, saying they wanted to travel to America to see Michael Jackson!
I was one of those sisters (Nodding head)
Yes, we got a visa to this land just like that!
It's almost like a joke, isn't it? (Looking at the audience and pause)
In spring of 1985, my sister and I set foot in America with $2,500 without a work permit. (Pause)

We knew some English and made a living doing various gigs every now
and then

In those days when I was desperate for a work permit, I called a friend
and asked:

"Hey, Hossein, do you know someone I could marry temporarily, just for
Green Card; someone I could divorce in no more than a year?"

He answered:

"You just find somebody willing to marry you, don't worry about filing
for divorce, he will leave you in six months anyway!"

I had so many good friends! (Smile)

It was hard to find a steady job without work permit

We lived day by day

At the end of the month we would set aside money for the next month's
rent

Buy a sack of rice and a few cans of tuna

And then pray to find work to carry us a little longer

My sister had an American boyfriend who kept telling us:

"You guys have to start from the bottom" (Serious deep voice)

"You guys have to start from the bottom"

He wouldn't understand when we told him we were children of privilege
and were not meant to work for a living!

We did our best to explain

BUT he just wouldn't understand

I didn't dare to tell him into his face but I used to mumble to myself:

> *Why don't you do right?*
> *Get out of here and get me some money too?*
> —Sang by Peggy Lee[5]

"Champaign taste, beer pocket" he would say (Soft smile)

He kept working on our pampered souls until my sister and I finally
accepted

Though reluctantly . . . (Looking incredulously)

That there's nothing shameful about working

Not even for us!

We tried a few restaurants for job

But they wouldn't hire anyone without experience

Until we saw this ad in a newspaper:

Waitress Wanted

Good Pay

No Experience Required (Smile)

We both dressed up and drove in our old, rusty, huge, white Chevrolet
that my cousin lent us to the address given in the paper

Though early in the afternoon, the restaurant's parking lot was full of
    snappy cars
Colorful and expensive
It was rather surprising for that time of the day
We looked around and soon noticed a pink neon sign flashing a half-
    naked woman with big curvy busts (Smile, looking incredulously)
The restaurant was actually a topless bar!
That is why they didn't require any experience!
We took a glance at the size of the neon busts . . .
And compared it with our own . . .
And realized that we are not qualified for this job either! (Shrugging
    shoulder)
We waited around the lot for half an hour, laughing our hearts out . . .
    (Pause)
Gradually, my sister and I got to know some Iranians in the city
And opportunities came up for part time work in various fields:
Sales, typing, advertising . . .
For a while we typed political books for Mahmood, an Iranian guy.
Though everything was in Farsi we couldn't make heads or tails of it.
All we knew was that Mahmood had communist political views
But . . . we were not worried
We thought, if the FBI ever arrested us
They could immediately tell how dumb we were about politics
And we have lots of respect for the capitalist system of the United States
    of America (Pause)
Another one of our memorable jobs was in a place where they altered
    Mercedes Benz cars for U.S. customs clearance
There couldn't be a worse experience
And I don't wish it on anyone
Our workplace was a mess!
Full of dust (Pause)
My sister and I didn't know if we were there to clean up or do office
    work!
The two-days-a-week we went there
We had to dig deep and clean up first, in order to find the desk and the
    dusty files to start our professional office work!
This was actually not so bad
The fun part was the hot and humid summer days of Houston, Texas,
Where we were surrounded by ants
They took such juicy bites out of our calves that we had to scratch day
    and night
Until our legs swelled like four fat eggplants (Pause)
The owners were two Iranian brothers

One of whom also managed a Burger King branch
Sometimes he came at noon with two whoppers and fries for us
We were so happy . . .
The joy of those treats stayed with us until payday (Pause)
At the end of the week, when the older brother was writing our check
The younger brother would stand there, saying:
How about the burgers?
Aren't you going to deduct the cost of the burgers from their paycheck?
My sister and I looked at each other
Calculating in our head what would be left out of our minimum wage of
    $3.25 an hour after deducting the cost of lunch! (Laughing at the old
    days)
These memories still bring laughter to our faces . . . (Pause)
You know . . .
In the first few years everything seemed possible, owing to our youth and
    energy
We could work in any condition
And get along with any employer
Hope for better days and youthful enthusiasm carried us along (Half
    smile, pause)
The pampered attitude had left our personalities as the realities of life
    jolted in
Finally, we realized that in order to taste the Champaign one has to work
    hard[6] (Pause)
I must admit that every now and then (Sad soft voice)
For years
I missed what my life was supposed to be like
I missed that feminine feeling and the need to lay my head on a masculine
    shoulder and rely on someone else.

Sometimes I need a shoulder to cry on
Someone strong to rely on
Someone to hold me in silence
Give me strength, hope and guidance
Someone to tell me not to worry
I'll take care of things what's your hurry?

Once, while I was working at a doctor's office
I called the attorney for one of our patients and told him his client is ready
    to be hospitalized.
The attorney was so glad to see his client had been taken care of and his
    work taken care of he, he asked:

"Ziba, what's your job in that office?"
"Nothing. I'm here to make life easy for you," I joked.

"Oh, my kind of girl!"

"I hate you and 'your kind of girls,'" I replied. "What happened to all
    those men who were supposed to take care of us?"
He laughed and said:

"I have bad news for you, Ziba"
"Those men are all dead!"

We ended the conversation laughingly
But later I kept thinking to myself, he is right
We . . . women like me . . . actually brought the end to those men
We wiped them out (Soft voice)
Grappling with the turbulent life as immigrants has occupied our minds
We had no choice but to learn how to survive on our own
In the process we became independent
Now we put on our suit every morning and leave home for work and no
    one dares to look down on us
Now it takes no one less than SUPERMAN himself to take care of us . . .
    (Three-second pause)
Years have passed since that day (Calm voice)
Now I'm more at peace with myself
I no longer feel that desperate need for that broad shoulder
I have learned to sing, dance and stomp through life
I'm happy that my man walks beside me like a comrade
Side by side (Pause)
Where there is a need
He takes a step forward to pave the way
And when he sees my long strides . . .
He steps aside and smiles with pride (Half smile)
I'm no longer hindered by those idle dreams
I have erased them from my mind . . .
And you know what?
I rid myself of confusing gender norms
Now I think to myself
"This is how life was meant to be . . . "
Everything was meant to happen exactly as it did . . . (Powerful voice)

> *I am me, a woman*
> *Freedom is what I wear*
> *Coquetry from my head to my toes*
> *But made of rock and steel*
> *I am me, a woman*
> *Comrade, friend, wife*
> *I am a mother*
> *O! You, who I fed, don't dare throw a veil on my head*

Sway of my hair is none but an illusion
none, but a vain image on the water
And these hadith of ruby lips and these intoxicating eyes
Are no more than whispers on the lips of a drunk
These accounts of bowed eyebrows and arrows of blackened eyelashes
is none, but weapons of poetic swagger
I am me, a woman
My figure bears fragrance of joyful delight
A Spark of life is within me, spawning with soul and spirit
O! You, the little fox! I am a lioness
you are darkness; I am the light
with means of divinity, don't set my fruition on fire, don't!
Thus you'd know my life and soul
extend a hand and aim to understand my role
O! You, the bitter piece!
Accept me as one with yours
I am of a different kind, but equal one with yours
Open your wings, and feathers, such is the way of love
and as such, I am a remix, if you are the wing of flight.[7]

NOTES

1. Readers should note that *italics* in the text represent singing by Ziba Shirazi who performed these as one-person shows. Unless otherwise noted, all poetry and lyrics quoted in the monologues and stories are original works by Ziba.

2. Ye Hong, "A Cultural Approach to Literature for Chinese Students," in *English and Globalization: Perspectives from Hong Kong and Mainland China*, ed. Kwok-kan Tam and Timothy Weiss (Hong Kong, China: Chinese University Press, 2004), drawing on the work of John Bodley has argued that culture involves at least three components: What people think, what they do, and the material products they produce (206). We have adapted this approach in the following manner: (1) What people think (In the above paragraph, Shirazi talks about the way she was thinking and was raised. She never thought of herself as a bread-earner; (2) What they do (culturally she was raised to be somebody's wife, like every other Iranian woman; even the well-educated ones); and (3) The material products they produce (urban middle-class women in Iran were raised to be housewives and if they worked it was to be part-time). Although as a young woman Shirazi used to work, she was never a bread-earner for her family. It was more of a hobby, or better to say, it was fashionable and a sign of modernity.

3. Raymond Williams introduces "the 'social' definition of culture, in which culture is a description of a particular way of life, which expresses certain meanings and values not only in art and learning but also in institutions and ordinary behavior," in his *The Long Revolution* (Ontario: Broadview Press, 1961), 57.

4. Poetry by Ziba Shirazi. Also note here, Victor Turner argues that stages of social drama involve a foregrounding of conflict that "seems to bring fundamental aspects of society, normally overlaid by the customs and habits of daily intercourse, into frightening prominence." People have to take sides in terms of deeply entrenched moral imperatives and constrains, often against their own personal preferences. Choice is overborne by duty" (Turner, *Drama, Fields and Metaphors: Symbolic Action in Human Society* [Ithaca, NY: Cornell University Press, 1974], 35).

5. Kansas Joe McCoy, "Why don't you do right," sung by Peggy Lee, (78 rpm records, A side) (New York: Columbia, 1942). See https://www.songfacts.com/lyrics/peggy-lee/why-dont-you-do-right (accessed October 26, 2019).

6. While growing up, we assumed men were in charge of providing for women. After migration we finally realized that in order to live in this land of opportunity, we had to adjust to the new rules of the western world. In this sense, our experience was similar to what Victor Turner calls a breach, the breaking of the rules of "norm-governed social life" (Turner, *From Ritual to Theatre: The Human Seriousness of Play* [Baltimore: PAJ Publications, 1982], 92).

7. Lyrics by Zibe Shirazi, "Zan," *Zananeha* (album) (Los Angeles: Shirazi, 1998). https://store.cdbaby.com/cd/zibashirazi10 (accessed October 28, 2019).

Two

The Outsider

Fariba Boghraty

(Setting: An old suitcase with a shawl over it in the middle of stage. A high stool, guitar on a guitar stand. Ziba picks up the shawl, warp around her shoulder and sits on the high stool.)

I was living in America before the revolution,
I had a green card
I was going to college then
Had a job
Living by myself and had my own apartment
Just like an American girl (Pause)
It was a year before the Islamic revolution when my mother came for a
 visit
The night before she was leaving for Iran
I held her and told her how much I love her
She calmly said: "If you really love me, you would come back to Iran."
I thought she is the most important person in my life and that I should do
 as she pleased
In less than a week I packed my suitcase and went back to Iran. (Pause)
Soon after, I found a job as a translator in an American accounting firm,
 where I met my husband Farrokh
He was my boss
BUT later on, I showed him who the real boss is! (Smile, three-second
 pause)
Farrokh was going to university
He had one more year before he could graduate.
We were dating for a year when I had to leave for America in order to
 validate my green card.

We were in love (Smile)
He called me
I called him
He called me
I called him
He called me
I didn't pick up the phone and came back to Iran and married him!
    (Smile)

> *I was in love with him from the beginning*
> *I am still in love with him*
> *First time I met him, I told myself*
> *I will stay with him till I die*

Farrokh was among many revolutionaries shouting "Down with America"
    and didn't want to move to America
I didn't mind living in Iran
But we were pushed out and forced to migrate by the new government
    and unexpected Islamic rules and regulations

> *O God, your name is being misused by many*
> *People are being killed under your name*
> *They are looting people's assets and rights*
> *Iran is becoming like a hell these days*

We were living in a three-story building in Jamaran, the same neighbor-
    hood as Ayatollah Khomeini! (Pause)
Every move we made was watched by militia guards
There was a checkpoint in the neighborhood, where they searched our car
    and, everything we carried in our handbags
From perfume to salt and pepper shakers
On top of it all, they put missiles on the rooftop to protect Khomeini and
    his neighborhood!

> *A man came calling himself the messenger of God*
> *Calling for people to die for him*
> *So, a tulip would grow on their graves*
> *No need to wash out their coffin*

It wasn't easy to be Khomeini's neighbor!
His militia guards thoroughly checked our visitors
God forbid our guests ever carry a wrapped gift box with breakables
    inside. . . .
They would have shaken the box so hard to the point of breaking whatev-
    er was inside
Many of our neighbors didn't last long (Pause)

Didn't take long for the second floor of our building to become a militia
    camp to protect Khomeini day and night.
We lasted four months . . .
In fact, we were the last ones to leave the building to the militia (Pause)
We left after they disconnected our electricity and everything in the freez-
    er spoiled, leaving an unbearable smell in the air for weeks
I couldn't believe what was happening . . .
It was as if these people were from another planet
I felt alienated

> *Come and sing with us the song of homesickness*
> *That we experienced in our own homeland*
> *Though we were from the same country*
> *We felt the alienation to the core*

We left that neighborhood for another
I remember once I was watering the lawn in front of our home . . .
When someone shouted,
"Don't you know there is water crisis and I can turn you to the authorities
    to imprison you for wasting water on the lawn?"
It was then when I told Farrokh,

"I refuse living in a country that I don't even know the laws of!"

Iran IS NOT my country anymore![1]

> *Goodbye happy days, Goodbye my homeland, tell me where the good days went*
> *Perhaps they can be found in stories or maybe they are gone forever*
> *As if no one is alive here, there is lots of crying, no time for laughter.*
>   —Ardalan Sarfaraz[2]

I left Iran for America
Soon after, I found a job and waited for Farrokh to come
He came six months later
My English was all right since I was living in California for a couple of
    years and went to school there
But Farrokh had problems with English (Smile)
He made up and improvised words that no one had ever heard of!
He didn't want to accept it either!
He somehow thought, because of his high-status job in Iran
He would lose status going to ESL classes in America! (Smile)
I was begging him to take ESL classes
He resisted, telling me

"I had taken English class in the university"
"I went to the consulate and got my visa without a translator"
"What I need is some time to find my way around"
"And learn English while living here and associating with non-Iranians!"

Finally, he gave in and we both went to ESL class.
I told the administrator that my husband is an educated man who had
     taken English classes at the university
And that he would like to take a test to see what level of English class he
     should be in
So, he won't be wasting his time (Smile)
The administrator agreed and started to ask him some questions:

"What is your name?"
"Farrokh."
"How old are you?"
"I am from Iran!"
"Are you married?"
"I came to America two weeks!"

"It shows! You should take English for the beginners!"
(Three-second pause)
I started working in a lab and, soon after, Farrokh joined me
The work environment was not pleasant at all
I stayed with them for about nine months
And I count those days as worst days of my life
Though the lab was owned by an Iranian, most of the employees were
     Chinese
We constantly had cultural clashes
Trying to say who is better![3] (Pause)
I quit my job first and then Farrokh followed my lead.

*[Fariba goes on about her maternity experience when she was at risk of
losing her life as well as her baby. She talks about her battle with cancer and
her way of handling it, as well as financial problems that she believes every
migrant faced. What she is most disappointed in is the way they were cheated
by Iranians, people from her own homeland. Towards the end of her interview she says:]*

Slowly life got better
And I opened my own office as an insurance agent
Farrokh joined me and we became a team
And we got nominated as the most successful insurance agency in Cali-
     fornia

          Good and bad days had passed
          The days that won't return
          Bitter or sweet, whatever it was
          I am happy that they passed
          The heavy burden of alienation has not broken our back
          All those bad memories

Became a cause for laughter these days

When I look at our life, I am content
My kids are happy and successful
We live a good life,
But I have to admit, migration is tough (Pause)
Sometimes I feel that I carried more than what I could stand on my back
Perhaps if we would have stayed in Iran
We could have gotten used to the Islamic Republic's restrictions and rules
    and would have had an easier life
Now I feel like an alien wherever I go.
When I go to Iran for visit,
I don't understand their slang.
Their language has changed a lot!
I can't connect with them anymore. (Pause)
After thirty years of living in America,
I don't belong to this country, either,
Nor does this country belong to me

> *This house is beautiful, but it is not my home*
> *This land is beautiful, but it is not my homeland*
> —K. Farshidvard[4]

[Fariba lost a homeland that could never be found.][5]

I wish I could have lived somewhere where I could proudly say
This is my country
I wish I didn't have to explain to everybody that I am from Iran
BUT against the Islamic Republic (Three-second pause)
I am tired of feeling alien
The only place I don't feel alienated is at home
With the kids and Farrokh

> *I yearned for simplicity and purity*
> *I yearned for someone who speaks my language*
> *I want everything exactly the way they were in old days*
> *I want the Old Persian days . . .*

NOTES

1. Stella Ting-Toomey argues that "cultural identity ... is defined as the emotional signifi-
cance we attach to our sense of belonging or affiliation with the larger culture" (Ting-Toomy,
Communicating Across Cultures [New York: Guilford Press, 1999], 30).

2. Ardalan Sarfaraz, "Bright Days" (1992), http://ardalan-sarfaraz.com/page-6.html (accessed October 26, 2019).

3. This may explain how theories of human communication account for the development of
prejudices towards others: Information-Integration Theory explores the ways we accumulate
and organize information about persons, objects, situations, and ideas to form attitudes or

predispositions, to act in a positive or negative way toward some object to make a judgment towards others (Stephen W. Littlejohn and Karen A. Foss, *Theories of Human Communication*, 9th ed. [Belmont, CA: Thomson Wadsworth, 2008], 75)

4. K. Farshidvard, "Salaye eshgh" (The call of love), in *Daftare sher* (Notebook of Poems), item number: 15066. Tehran: Omide Majd, 2002. https://shop.ketab.com/book-detail.aspx?item =15066&title =%D8%B5%D9%84%D8%A7%DB%8C%20%D8%B9%D8%B4%D9%82&au thor=%D9%81%D8%B1%D8%B4%D9%8A%D8%AF%D9%88%D8%B1%D8%AF%D8%8 C%20%D8%AE%D8%B3%D8%B1%D9%88 (accessed October 28, 2019).

5. "Crossing cultures can be a stimulating and rewarding adventure. It can also be a stressful and bewildering experience" (Colleen A. Ward, Stephen Bochner, and Adrian Furnham, *The Psychology of Culture Shock*, 2nd ed. [Philadelphia: Taylor & Francis, 2001], i).

Three

The Pain of Language Barrier

Farrokh Boghraty

(Setting: An old suitcase in the middle of stage. Wooden coat rack hanger on stage with a green tie hanging on one of the hooks, a high stool, guitar on a guitar stand. Ziba comes on stage wearing a men's shirt, shouting, has anybody seen my green tie? Finds it and pick it up from the coat rack: Ah . . . here, I knew I put it somewhere safe! Ziba puts the tie loosely around her neck and sits on the high stool.)

> *I know what it's like to be an outsider, a kharejee.* [1]
> *I know how English sounds*
> *when every word is only music*
> *I know how it feels not*
> *to be an American, an English, a French*
> *Call them*
> > *Amrikayee, Inglessee, Faransavi*
> *see them*
> > *See me as alien, immigrant, Iranee.*
> *But I've been here so long*
> *they may call me American*
> > *with an American husband*
> > *and American children . . .*
> *But mark this—I do not belong anywhere.*
> *I have an accent in every language I speak*
> > > > —Sholeh Wolpe [2]

My name is Farrokh. Here, they call me *Fred*.
For a long time, they called me *Frock*!
A friend of mine told me to change my name to Fred
So that Americans could pronounce my name!
At the beginning, I didn't respond to Fred
Many times my co-worker asked,

"Aren't you Fred?"
"Yes I am." (Soft voice)
"Then how come you don't respond?"

I have been *Farrokh* all my life!
Now my name becomes a problem in this foreign land!

> *My name was with me for years*
> *It was given to me by my father*
> *It was the name I memorized*
> *Like my shadow, my name was always with me*
> *Within a day it changed here*
> *Because it caused me problems*

I was going to the university in Iran before the Islamic Revolution
And I was politically active
I walked with a million others in every pro-Khomeini demonstration
I even guarded my neighborhood with a gun! (Pause)
Rumor had it that, there were people who attacked neighborhoods to cut throats and rape women!
Once, it was my turn to guard the neighborhood along with Varuj,
The Armenian man in the neighborhood
I was twenty-six and Varuj was forty.
The first thing we did was to make a shield to stand behind by piling many sand bags on top of two chairs
The neighbors were treating us with tea, sweets, and fruits until two o'clock in the morning
Slowly, the neighborhood quieted down (Low voice)
The lights went off and everybody went to sleep
We were talking in whispers about Khomeini and his great promises and the change that was about to happen
Until suddenly we heard a noise and noticed something jump on the sand bags!
Right away we both dropped our guns and put our hands up! (Both hands up)
We were so afraid (Pause)
It took us about 10 seconds to pull ourselves together and turn around to see the weak, tiny, yellow neighborhood cat
Looking at us carelessly (Careless look)
It meowed and left
We pulled our hands down quietly and said nothing
Both knowing how weak we were in front of the so-called enemy! (Pause)
What else did you expect from the people who had seen Khomeini's face in the moon?[3]

[Farrokh's story continues with many unexpected bitter and tragic incidents as the result of the revolution. Eventually he and his wife Fariba decide to leave Iran. Since Fariba had a Green Card, she came to America and waited for Farrokh.]

I was referred to an American accounting firm by the company I was working with in Iran.

I obtained my U.S. visa in Italy with no difficulties

And I entered the United States at the airport in NY

I walked to the checkpoint carrying nothing but a briefcase and an overcoat!

They asked me,

"Do you have any luggage?"

"No," I said (Calmly)

"I just came to sign a contract and go back to Iran."

I couldn't tell them that I came with two huge bags filled with Persian crafts, a five-year supply of saffron and Persian delights to sign a contract and leave! (Pause)

You know, Americans are very civilized

If you tell them that you don't have luggage they don't tell you that you are lying

They send your luggage to the door in ten days

No questions asked![4] (Three- second pause)

The minute I walked into this country

I told myself that this is the land of opportunities

One must become Christopher Columbus and discover the best.

Soon I registered in ESL class for free and paid only 50 cents for books (Pause)

During lunch break I went out to see what is going on at the school

I found a food truck in the middle of the school

Giving away water, sodas and sandwiches.

I saw people lining up and taking whatever, they wished

So I got myself coffee with sugar and cream, thinking to myself

"What a country! You can go to school with fifty cents and they serve free coffee!"

The second night I saw the truck again

I thought to myself

"Now that everything is free, why not have my dinner here?"

So I picked a hotdog

Dressed it with ketchup, mustard

AND to treat myself well . . . added a soda.

To change my view, I decided to go to the other side of the truck
There, I notice another line where people were lining up to pay for the
    things they picked up from the other side of the truck!
I thought to myself, trust is such a valuable thing![5] (Three- second pause)
I went to ESL classes during the night and worked during the day
I was told by my English teacher that, whenever I didn't understand what
    someone was saying
I should say, "Excuse me," at least at first
If I still I couldn't understand them, I should ask the person to spell out
    the word for me (Pause)
Once at work my boss told me to pick up the phone and talk to Mr.
    Anderson
I was to get his address to send him a check
I picked up the phone and firmly said

"Good morning Mr. Anderson. How are you? Can I have your address?"

He kindly, but quickly, responded

"1100 Smith Street, Pacific Palisades, CA 90272"

Since I didn't understand I calmly said

"Excuse me?"

He repeated it as fast as he had the first time

"1100 Smith Street, Pacific Palisades, CA 90272"

Since I didn't understand him for the second time
And remembered what my English teacher had told me
I casually asked

"Would you spell it for me?"

I didn't hear anything after that
Mr. Anderson hung up the phone on me!
A couple of minutes later my boss came in and asked me to hand him Mr.
    Anderson's check so he could mail it out himself! (Shaking head)
Not knowing the language needs its own chapter in a book.

> *I got used to Persian language and accent,*
> *I who knew the answer to every question*
> *Now is like a baby who just started to talk,*
> *Alas, I can't even finish my sentence . . .*
>   —Hadi Khorsandi[6]

There are many shared words between Farsi and the English language
    such as "mother"
In Farsi, we say *mādar*.

And for "brother" we say *Barādar.*
For "taxi," we have the same word
With a different pronunciation (tāxi)
We also have many French words shared with Farsi such as
Bronchit for bronchitis
Which I didn't know the origin of . . .
Having said all this
I remember in the early days of migration
I caught a cold and was coughing so badly that I had to see a doctor
I called the doctor's office for an appointment
And the secretary asked

"What is your reason for seeing the doctor?"

I replied:

"I have brown shit!"

I thought to myself that since *bronchit* is not a Persian word
If I give it an American accent it would be English!
She shockingly asked again

"What is your reason sir?"

I juiced up my accent and repeated

"I have brown shit!"

Reluctantly, she gave me an appointment (Half smile)
It was after seeing the doctor that I found out the English word for *bronchit* is Bronchitis!
Oh, the pain of the language barrier!

> *I have a charming accent in Persian,*
> *Taking care of my needs,*
> *communicating with no difficulties*
> *Slowly, I learned "hello" "please," Few words, here and there*
> *I talked like a newborn, Couldn't say a word, mute, dumb*
> —Hadi Khorsandi[7]

For years, I was doing bookkeeping for an Iranian businessman named
Mr. Ahmadi who was in the rug business
To make life easy for him
I asked Mr. Ahmadi to keep a daily journal of his finances
A memoire about money!
He wrote down every transaction
Whether he paid or received
Then, at the end of the month I transcribed the transactions into books
For example, he wrote: (Clear voice)

August 12, 1989: I gave $320.00 to my wife for household items

August 14, 1989: I gave $345.96 to John for office supplies

August 18, 1989: Sold the red carpet to George for $1500.00 and etc. . . .

One thing I noticed was that every month he also paid for "Visa"

Every month he wrote Visa $180.00 or $220.00 and so on . . .

I also noticed that the amount paid never exceeded $250.00

Since all my friends and family were dreaming about obtaining a visa and coming to America, I truly admired Mr. Ahmadi for getting a visa each month for one of his family members and bringing them all into the United States! (Pause)

It took me a while to realize that by "Visa" he meant the credit card! (Half smile and shaking head)

It took me years to adjust to this country and learn about living in America

I had so many difficulties learning the American culture and the English language

> *The pain of language barrier*
> *As if it will never ease*
> *The pain of language barrier*
> —Hadi Khorsandi[8]

Along with my wife Fariba

We faced many ups and downs in life, like every immigrant . . . (Sad voice)

Our best friends cheated us over money . . .

Our closest family member stabbed us in the back

Our own Iranian fellows took advantage of us for not being familiar with the system

But, thank God, we overcame all of the difficulties

> *Everybody had his/her own way to break our heart,*
> *Friends in one way, enemies in another way*
> *Being heartbroken by an enemy does not bother me,*
> *Ask my friends, why they broke my heart?*
> —Nahid Yousefi[9]

I was working in a laboratory for a while

I learned my biggest life lesson while working there.

Since Fariba and I were new to the U.S

My friend told us that we had to go see Las Vegas

I replied

"But I am new at my job and I don't have any days off"

He said

"Take it easy. Call in sick or tell them your father passed! Nothing will happen!"

Thursday morning, I called in my manager and with a sad voice told him that my father had just passed away

I said I was devastated and couldn't come to work!

He deeply sympathized with me and told me to take time off work

I was so happy about fooling him so easily!

Joyfully, we left for Las Vegas with our friends for four days! (Smile)

While in Vegas I learned something new!

As I was walking on the street, someone came close to me asking if I wanted coke

Since I had never heard of nor used anything but Coca Cola

I thought to myself, "What a country!

What caring people!

They see it is hot, they offer you coke!

Since I wasn't thirsty myself

I shouted out to my friend who was walking a bit ahead of me

"Ali this guy is asking if you want coke"

The guy disappeared in a second

And Ali told me about a different kind of coke! (Pause)

It was a great trip and we had so much fun

I came back to work on Monday

My manager came to my desk

Offered me his condolences

And handed me an envelope

I asked him

"What is this?"

He replied

"It is our company's policy, that whoever loses his family gets three days off and $1000.00."

You have one more day off

If you feel you are not ready to work you can have today off as well

I was so happy thinking that not only had I fooled them, BUT I also got $1000.00! (Pause)

It took me *TEN* years to realize what an uncivilized person I had been for telling that lie (Loud but timid voice)

It took me *TEN* years to realize my mistake.

It took me *TEN* years to get rid of my prejudice

And to genuinely evaluate myself,

My culture,

My values,

And my beliefs.
It took me *TEN* years to realize the positive aspects of living in the
     Western world. (Three-second Pause)
Now, I am happy about my migration. (Smile)
I appreciate and like the fact that this country is so diverse.
I feel like the whole world is within a ten-mile radius of my home.
The neighborhood bakery is Korean,
The restaurant owner is French,
The grocery store is owned by a Mexican, and . . . (Three-second pause)
I came to believe that you are given only one chance to come to this world
To live your life
Do your best and choose the best
I have made two great choices in my life,
The second one was coming to America.
Are you wondering about the first?
It was, of course, marrying Fariba, my wife!
She is the best choice I have ever made in my life.
She has always been here for me
And trusted me with the choices I have made in life for all of us.
We shared the best and the worst
We shared the happiest and the saddest days of our life
Yes, she is my best choice in life

> *My first love, timeless love*
> *My wife, my best friend*
> *Without you I am lonely, you complete me*
> *Patient in hard days*
> *My wife, my friend, my fellow traveler*
> *I love you, with all my heart*

NOTES

1. foreigner.
2. Sholeh Wolpe, "The Outsider," In *Rooftops of Tehran: Poems* (Pasadena, CA: Red Hen Press, 2008), 82.
3. See the discussion of this in chap. 2., "From the Moon to Television: A Story of the Iranian Revolution of 1979," Shahla Talebi writes: "as millions of Iranians awaited for the return of Ayatollah Khomeini from exile, a rumor swept the country that his face could be seen in the moon; and thanks to modern technology, the rumor soon reached almost every corner of the country" (*International Society for Iranian Studies*, conference paper 8th Biennial Conference on Iranian Studies, Association for Iranian Studies,. May 27–30, 1996, Santa Monica, CA).
4. David B. Buller and Judee K. Burgoon's "Interpersonal Deception Theory," *Communication Theory* 6, no. 3 (1996): 203–42, is relevant here: "a message knowingly transmitted by a sender to foster a false belief or conclusion by the receiver" and it can be a lie, partially telling the truth or intentionally vague (205).

5. Expectancy Value theories of motivation stress two key cognitive influences: People's judgments about the likelihood of success at a task (expectancies) and their reasons for engaging in the task (values)" (Andrew J. Elliot and Carol Dweck, *Handbook of Competence and Motivation* [New York: Guilford Press, 2007], 90). The general idea is that there are expectations as well as values or beliefs that affect subsequent behavior.

6. Hadi Khorsandi, "Bogzar az ney" (Let go of the flute) (May 4, 1998), https://iranian.com/Satire/May98/khorsandi.html?site=archive (accessed October 28, 2019).

7. Khorsandi, "Bogzar az ney."

8. Khorsandi, "Bogzar az ney."

9. Nahid Yousefi, "Harkas be tarighi del e ma mishekanad" (Each one has a unique way of breaking our hearts) (n.d.), https://ayateghamzeh.ir/Poem/ID/107834/%D9%87%D8%B1-%DA%A9%D8%B3-%D8%A8%D9%87-%D8%B7%D8%B1%DB%8C%D9%82%DB%8C-%D8%AF%D9%84-%D9%85%D8%A7-%D9%85%DB%8C-%D8%B4%DA%A9%D9%86%D8%AF (accessed October 26, 2019).

Four

Senior Life

Massy Alavi

(Setting: An old suitcase with a shawl over it in the middle of stage. A high stool, guitar on a guitar stand. Ziba picks up the shawl, warp around her shoulder and sits on the highchair.)

In Iran, once I was shouting along with a million others

Bakhtiar, Bakhtiar, sangareto negahdar! (Hands up, powerfully demon-
    strating and shouting)
Bakhtiar Bakhtiar hold on to your barricades!
Encouraging the Prime Minister Bakhtiar
NOT to give up his position and give into the Islamic Republic.
When I came home
It was in the news that he had fled the country to Paris!
From then on, I didn't get involved in revolution and politics

> *I stood up for him, shouting in his defense*
> *But, he was already gone!*
> *I put my life on the line for him, ready to die*
> *But, he was already gone!*
> *I was ready to sacrifice all at hand*
> *But, he was already gone!*
> *He had fled ahead, leaving us all behind*
> *He was already gone!*

I was a high school teacher and principal in Iran when the Islamic Repub-
    lic came to power
The education department called on principals to dictate to them what to
    say about the revolution!
I thought to myself

There is no place for me in a country where someone has to dictate to me
   what to say. (Pause)
My husband Changiz, had been working in the justice department for
   over thirty-three years
I asked him to retire so we could join our son in the U.S. for good.
As for myself,
I applied for a long-term vacation
The department of education didn't accept my request
I was told:
"Presently we need you here; otherwise we would have fired you our-
   selves!"

> *My principles stood in my way*
> *Tied my hands and caused my dismay*

My son, who was receiving his master's degree, sent us an invitation from
   the U.S.
My husband had a multiple entry visa to the U.S.
I thought, by God's will I get my visa as well. (Pause)
So, I went to the department of education in Tehran
I asked the person in charge: Are you Muslim?
Yes, he said
I replied: I am Muslim too
This is an invitation from my son in America
My husband told me:
"If you want to come with me . . . come . . . if not . . . I am leaving . . .
   goodbye . . . divorce!"
What do you think I should do as a Muslim woman?
He raised his eyebrow, started thinking and said:
"Go sister . . . go, apply for leave of absence and accompany your hus-
   band. BUT come back more committed and more competent for the
   Islamic Republic."

> *In my desperation to leave*
> *I said things that I didn't believe*
> *In my longing to leave and set myself free*
> *I wove a wing to fly high and flee*

My husband Changiz and I entered Austin, Texas in May of 1979
I had a bachelor's degree in English in Iran
I could speak English.
Immediately I went to Saint Edward University and registered in their
   Social Work Program
Got my certificate and started being trained at a Senior Center as a volun-
   teer. (pause)
To tell you the truth I never had the intention of going back to Iran

But my husband Changiz had his ticket to go back on November 7th, 1979

Three days before his departure on November 4th, 1979 the hostage crisis happened in Iran

Everybody told him: "Changiz don't go to Iran in this situation."

He replied: "No worries, they will free the hostages tomorrow; and I will be back soon."

They kept the hostages for 444 days and he couldn't come back to the U.S. for over two years!

> *He left on his own will*
> *He could return only by God's will*
> *There was no other way*
> *But to pray to God night and day*

At the time of the hostage crisis an American friend of mine suggested that I write a letter to the families of the hostages

I did, he translated it into English

The English version was printed in the *Daily Texan* newspaper on June 26, 1980

And the Persian version in *Iran Times*

Here . . . I have a copy of it . . . (show newspaper)

In short, I wrote:

"As an Iranian woman and mother and a representative of thousands of Iranian families such as my own, I am writing this letter to all of you who have loved ones held captive in my country. I understand and feel your pain and suffering, But please understand that we have taken refuge in your country out of fear for our lives."

I asked them to consider us as individual human beings, not as persons from that distant land whose name is a cause of frustration and anger for many Americans.

At the end I asked them not to put the crimes of others on our doorstep[1] (Pause)

Because of that letter I was granted political asylum, and got my green card

> *How great it is to sympathize in sad times*
> *Our voice will echo in the world*
> *Only if you and I join in accord*

My son moved to New Jersey and we followed him

I thought that since I had teaching experience it would be wise to study early childhood education.

I had four units to finish my diploma when my counselor told me that
    because of my accent they could not give me my diploma! (Wonder-
    ing look)
I said:
"And now you are telling me?"
He said:
"Listen to me Massy, you can teach in middle school or high school."
"You can even teach at a university,"
"But not kindergarten!"
"Because you have an accent!"
He asked me:
"Would you like an American teacher to teach your five-or-six-year-old
    child Persian with an American accent?!"
There was logic behind what he was saying . . . (Acceptance nodding)
He made sense, but it was too late!
I told him:
"I wish you had told me this at the beginning!"
They handed me my diploma reluctantly and I worked under another
    teacher for three years

> *I was happy so long as I was around books,*
> *Teaching and school*
> *Feeling fortunate so long as education was my tool*

Everything was going well till my husband Changiz had a brain stroke!
He was in a coma for four months
I went through tough times . . .
And I wasn't the only one
Marshmallow, our cat, who was always sitting on Changiz's books dis-
    turbing him and preventing him from reading, was as sad and as
    depressed as I was.

> *My husband, my companion, my fellow traveler*
> *My other half, my best friend, my partner,*
> *He left and I am all alone*
> *With a lifetime of memories,*
> *Laughter and joy are no longer in me, it seems*

Two years later, I sold the house in New Jersey and moved to California
    with Marshmallow
I rented an apartment and got two part time jobs
One in a Montessori in Irvine and another in a department store in Fash-
    ion Island
I liked California
Especially because wherever I went, there was an Iranian
I remember once I was lost

I stopped at an intersection and pulled down the window and asked the
    driver how to get to Jamboree?
The lady sitting next to the driver, said, " I guess she is Iranian let me tell
    her."
(*Fekr konam Iraniye, begzar man behesh begam*)

> *Oh! What joy to hear a familiar voice in exile*
> *Oh! What joy to be touched by a kind heart in exile*
> *Though my host country embraces me with a smile*
> *It is home that I long for once in a while*

Life was good, until Marshmallow had a heart attack because she was
    overweight!
I was heartbroken, crying, dressing in black and mourning for a long time
During that time, I met an elderly lady who had just come from Iran to
    live with her daughter
She was homesick, crying day and night wishing to go back to Iran.
There was another crying lady who just lost her husband
The three of us decided to have coffee in Fashion Island
The first week we sat together . . . we had so much fun (Smile)
So we planned for the week after . . .
Again we had so much fun, so, we planned for the week after . . .
I put my training as a social worker to work and told the ladies to bring a
    friend with them for the next meeting
Every week we had a new person added to our group

> *Should God close a door on your destined journey,*
> *Another door he will open out of mercy*
> *Spring blossomed in my heart anew*
> *The smile on my face was again joyful and true*

When our number got to twelve, I thought we cannot sit at a coffee shop
    in a mall . . .
Everybody is looking at us!
It was 1995
Lakeview Senior Center had just opened
We all took our lunch to the center
Every nationality was sitting quietly at a table having lunch . . .
Fourteen of us sat at the table for eight!
All of us offering food and *taarof*-ing food to one another
Talking, laughing and having a great time . . .
The director of the center came and asked who we were
I told her we are homesick Iranian mothers getting together

> *A darling mother far from her roots, displaced and sad*
> *Sits alone homesick dreaming of her dear homeland*
> *Her deep-felt longing stirring hearts all around, touching and true*

Fragrant and sweet
Like the scent of a homeland she once knew

—Massy[2]

She said,

"If your number rises to thirty you will be identified as a club and I can
    give you a room."

Right away I made a flyer and left it at every place I could think of

From grocery stores to hair salons

I wrote:

"Dear Iranian . . . if you are homesick and would like to meet someone
    from your own homeland, come and join us."

Around I went meeting and greeting
Was welcomed with open hearts,
Willing and giving

—Massy[3]

Slowly our number got to forty

A Persian radio interviewed me and Abdol-Ali Homayoun known as
    Sarkar Ostovar, the famous Iranian TV personality, came to help me

Every Thursday after lunch we pushed back the tables

Played music, sang and danced . . . had a lot of fun

From the day we met and gathered in union
We vowed to stay together, a loyal companion
My heart lightens in your dear presence
Enriched day after day in joyful existence

—Massy[4]

Everything was going well when the director called me and said:

Massi, your group disturbed our system (Serious voice)

The room you gather in belongs to everybody AND it has to be used as a
    classroom to learn things NOT to party all the time! I give you a week
    to clear the room after lunch

But you can get together one night a week

We were deeply saddened (Sad voice and face)

Ghame donya oomad to delemoon. The sadness of the whole world came
    to our heart

You know . . . Iranian immigrants of those days were different from now

Today's immigrants are mostly educated, they speak English. They are
    more familiar with the system.

They emigrated in the hope of making a better future for themselves and
    their children.

But those days immigrants were parents who followed their successful
    educated children

Most of them didn't speak English and were not familiar with the system

They were lonely and felt out of place[5] (Pause)

So I talked to the director. I said, " You see there is a support group for those who face trauma in any way, for those whose homes caught on fire

Those who lost a loved one

Those who face a life-threatening sickness . . .

We have faced a trauma too; we lost our homeland (Sad voice)

We have no one to talk with in our language, these gatherings are like a support group for us.

> *We have lost our children, we have been through heartache*
> *Like an empty vase on the window sill, we are full of broken memories*
> —Gh. Aminpour[6]

Finally, they gave us a room

But . . . You know how Iranians are!?

We asked for more!

We told them because we need too much support, we need a room for both daytime and nighttime!

Fortunately, they agreed. (Smile, Three-second pause)

I retired myself and wholeheartedly volunteered and did as much as I could for the center.

It has been about twenty years now that I take care of things with the help of other ladies at the center.

Every Thursday we get together from two to four in the afternoon (Cheerful voice)

Minimum seventy people show up . . .

We have poetry reading . . .

People bring articles to read

Every third Thursday of the month we gather at five in the afternoon

We have music

Artists voluntarily come and perform for us . . . it is fun (Three-second pause)

In 2005, The Orange County Human Relations Commission awarded me for gathering Iranians

This was the first time ever that an Iranian was awarded

They projected lights on me till I got to the podium

I wasn't ready at all . . . I don't even have a decent picture! (Shy face)

The next day a senator sent me a letter . . .

It was published in the newspaper...

I still cannot believe I was awarded for doing something that I enjoyed so much

> *I did whatever I could whole-heartedly*
> *Though I was weak*

I did my best undoubtedly

I am happy about my migration . . .

Happy living in this country . . .

I flew as high as I could and took advantage of every opportunity given to
me.

And to show my appreciation, whenever and wherever I feel there is a
need for me

I volunteer and work.

I never get tired of volunteer work. Never!

In fact, I am getting younger and younger! (Smile)

NOTES

1. Hamid Naficy, *The Making of Exile Cultures: Iranian Television in Los Angeles* (Minne-apolis: University of Minnesota Press, 199), has argued that the hostage crisis caused a "double exclusion" and "dual marginality," meaning that "the exiles were accepted neither at home nor in exile" (131). See the discussion of Hamid Naficy's seminal work on Iranian Diaspora in chap. 1.

2. Throughout this chapter, all poems by Massy (whose story this is) where given to Ziba Shirazi in writing at the time of their interview, November 2014, Irvine, California; Massy's works are unpublished.

3. Massy, interview with Shirazi, November 2014, Irvine, California, unpublished.

4. Massy, interview with Shirazi, November 2014, Irvine, California, unpublished.

5. Newcomers often become involved in activities with their co-ethnics or co-nationals to organize mass communication outlets. "Through a wide range of mediated communication system such as radio, television, newspaper, magazine, movie, art, literature, music and drama, non-natives interact with their host cultural milieu without direct interpersonal involvement" (*The Routledge Handbook of Language and Intercultural Communication*, ed. Jane Jackson [New York: Routledge, 2013], 236).

6. Gh. Aminpour, "Goldan-e Khali" (Empty vase), (n.d.). http://shereno.com/poet-33 40.html (accessed October 26, 2019).

Five

Lost Identity

Nasrin Almasi

(Setting: An old suitcase in the middle of stage. A high stool and a guitar on stand.)

> *There are many stories*
> *Stories of willows and wind*
> *The wind blew and shocked my core*
> *But my roots stood firm as before*

When the Islamic Republic took over in Iran,
My husband, Hassan, and I were among the first to be dismissed from our teaching positions as part of the Cultural Revolution.
They said Hassan was an apostate, and they convicted him of the Islamic verdict of "corruption on earth," which is the Sharia law's equivalent of a death sentence. (Pause)
We were forced to leave our province for Tehran.
For a while, we lived in hiding,
Until we finally decided to leave Iran.
First Hassan left.
He easily got his U.S. visa and settled in Los Angeles
Where he waited for us.
Following him,
Our two daughters, Sara, age seven, and Sahar, age five, and I headed for Turkey.
In the hopes of getting a U.S. visa, we stayed in Turkey for a full year. (Pause)
Turkey would only issue visas for three months at a time.
We had to leave Turkey for Yugoslavia every three months,
Stay overnight and come back to the border

In order to renew our Turkish visa for another three months.
Finally, we made contact with a smuggler
Who promised to get us a U.S. visa.
I was so naïve (Timid voice)
Without any question,
I gathered the money he asked for and handed it to him.
He got us a visa for Italy
Then he gave me a piece of paper with a name and address
And told me

"You go to this person. He will get you a U.S. visa in Italy!"

We left . . .
When we entered Italy
There, I realized that the visa didn't include the girls!
And my girls are not allowed to enter Italy!
I am still amazed at my reaction at the time (guitar strumming couple of
    cords with tension)
I still don't know where my strength came from?! (Loud strained voice)
I became a tigress whose children were about to be taken away from her
    (Louder)
In any way that I could (Louder)
Using body language,
Speaking, half Persian, half English
I cried (crying voice)
I screamed
I hollered
I begged
Finally I made them understand that I would not be separated from my
    daughters . . . NOT EVEN FOR A MOMENT . . . (Sudden strum and
    stop)

> *Gray hair may be a sign of old age at first sight*
> *But it was trauma that aged me overnight*
> *—Masoud Sepand*[1]

Finally, and mercifully, after several hours (Dropping voice)
They issued visas for the kids and the three of us entered Rome.

> *Speak your truth*
> *Even if your voice may not reach a soul*
> *Sometimes, truth cuts like the edge of a sword*
> *—Masoud Sepand*[2]

It was late at night
I didn't know anyone or anyplace in Rome
We took the bus to the city and spent the night in a Motel.

Our lives were thrown into a tailspin
Our pains about to begin
The incurable pain of exile
The pain of loneliness and fear

The next day

With the ultimate naiveté, I went to the address that the smuggler had
    given us

That address didn't even exist . . . (Sad voice)

But I didn't want to believe that

I kept trying to convince myself

Maybe if I don't find it today

For sure I will find it tomorrow

Now, I laugh at my own stupidity (Quiet soft laugh)

How simple-minded can one be? (Pause)

The smuggler had promised us that two days after our entry into Italy we
    would be heading for America.

We spent a few nights in the motel

We didn't have much money left

And I didn't have the heart to tell Hassan that we had lost all our money!

I could neither go forward nor back

I had no choice but to move into a train station

Where the homeless stayed at night.

> *Gray hair may be a sign of old age at first sight*
> *But, it was trauma that aged me overnight*
> —Masoud Sepand[3]

I went early in the afternoon to find a good place . . .

Somewhere less windy

So the girls wouldn't get cold . . .(Pause)

The station was crowded

With thousands of people in motion

Suddenly I heard someone speaking Persian

Once again, the same strength overtook me (Loud voice)

As if it were not my own (Louder)

I stood in the middle of the train station and shouted with all my strength:
    (Louder)

> *Is there an Iranian here*
> *to ra be khoda be man begid inja irani hast?*
> *For goodness sake* (Crying voice)
> *Tell me! Is there an Iranian here?*

Suddenly a man turned around

I ran towards him (Speaking fast)

In less than five minutes, I told him all that had happened

> *I spoke of me and you and us*
> *I spoke of the world across*
> *I spoke of tough days*
> *Of cold nights and of dismay*

The same night he put me in touch with an organization in which Iranians were helping refugees.

> *Hold my hand, for you know my pain, don't linger on or hesitate in vain*
> *Love of my country and countryman calls me, It is their kindness that binds me*
> —Masoud Sepand[4]

Someone came and paid for our motel
And the day after with the help of the organization we were placed in a home and applied for political asylum . . .
Which is another story . . . (Pause)
The Italian government would say
Because your husband is in the U.S. you have to apply from there
The American government would say because . . . (Trailing off)
Uh . . . this story can wait for another time... (Distressed voice)

> *There are many stories*
> *Stories of willows and wind*
> *The wind blew and shocked my core*
> *But my roots stood firm as before*

The girls and I stayed in Italy for more than a year.
I weighed only eighty-five pounds...
I had no money to eat
If I could get ahold of any food, I would give it to the girls
Sometimes, for a few days, I wouldn't eat anything . . .
Not even a piece of bread
A few times, I almost fainted from the scent of food when passing by a restaurant
We lived with the bare minimum (Pause)
The only thing that was available to the girls in abundance was love
Many times, all three of us slept on a bed with no mattress
Covering ourselves with a blanket
The girls' food was only bread and beans once a day
And on special occasions twice a day
My food depended on my financial situation
I remember once, a group of Iranians invited us to a feast that was thrown in honor of the Afghan ambassador.
There were many kinds of food on display
My daughter, seeing all this food, (Half smile)
Pulled at my skirt and asked

"Mom . . . Mom . . . do we eat our beans and bread first or after eating this food?!" (little girl voice)

Poor kid had eaten bread and beans for so long
That she thought it didn't matter what was served
The beans and bread were mandatory! (Short laugh)
Now I laugh about it
But back then . . . I shed countless tears . . .

> *Yesterday's sorrow is today's laughter*
> *Yesterday's pain is today's banter*
> *Amidst endless tears I round my way*
> *I spread my wings to fly far and away*

Thankfully, our asylum application started moving forward and we were able to use social services and assistance
I thought,
Maybe I should find another job to make up for all the hardships that the girls had been through
I started selling newspapers at intersections
I remember the first day (Sad voice)
I went to work at 3 o'clock in the afternoon
Took the newspapers and started work at 4 PM
As I was standing at the intersection . . .
Suddenly I felt that my hands were wet and my body was hot...
I realized that for hours I had been standing at the intersection motionless
JUST crying

> *Hopeless days of hardship were plenty*
> *I had to bear the pain without breaking,*
> *Anger at the world unjust*
> *Tears were shed in thrust*

Since I had to give a percentage of my sales for the day to my employer, I had to bear a lot of criticism that day. . . .
But from that day on, I began to take work seriously
And slowly but surely fell into the rhythm.
The income was good
The girls started school and their Italian improved
Mine however, didn't improve much
Because I was mostly in contact with Iranians
To repay for all the help that was given to us,
I opened my door to other refugees and accepted them with open arms,
Believe it or not, in the midst of all the difficulties (Smiling and talking)
Along with some other Iranians
I brought one of Bertolt Brecht's *The Chalk Cross* on stage

In order to remind myself of my own identity[5]
It was an interesting experience. . . .

> *Days and nights went by*
> *Through good and bad we held our heads up high*
> *Alas! My youth is gone*
> *Of it there is left none*

For almost three years, Hassan and I lived apart from one another
Our refugee status stalled in both Italy and the U.S.
Hassan left for Canada
After a short while
With a little more caution
We found another smuggler who brought the girls and me to Canada
AND finally in 1987
Canada accepted us as immigrants.
I have to say
At first in Canada, everything and everyone felt horribly strange
I felt disconnected even from my husband Hassan
In fact, all of us were in a daze!
You know, three years of separation and living in two foreign lands had
    changed me a lot.
I had learned new things (Confident voice)
I had seen new social relations and different ways of social interaction
In Iran, I had learned to be a good wife
I had to show love and be ready for many selfless sacrifices...
In the West
I learned about the equality of men and women
I became familiar with women's equal rights in the home, in love, and in
    all aspects of life
Feminist concepts had grown and taken root in me
My views on life and my dreams had changed
Each day (Stronger voice)
My social and cultural identity became clearer
Stronger
And brighter.
Hassan and I lived together for five or six months as two strangers
To the point that
If I wanted to change the location of an object in our bedroom
I didn't know if it was okay to do so
Since Amir had placed it there!
Or . . . if it were ok for me to open his drawers!
Something that in marital relationship happens effortlessly
Where husband and wife share access to everything!

I could see quite clearly that Hassan was also feeling lost
And felt that he didn't know this woman anymore
AND rightly so . . . (Powerful voice)
For that kind
Delicate
Soft
And patient woman he once knew had transformed
Into a woman who now strongly put her foot down and called out:

"I" (Loud)

It took a while
Slowly we warmed up to each other
And I got to know him all over again.
I could see how hard he tried to shed his outdated male-centric skin of
    old . . .
And how much he wanted to strengthen the foundations of our relation-
    ship
And I greatly valued his effort. (Soft voice)
I have to say
I fell in love with him all over again
Now
Even deeper than before. . . .

> *With you I became myself again*
> *I fell in love with my body and soul again,*
> *With you, I blossomed like a flower*
> *With you, I became a woman again*

It was a grueling period of our lives . . .
Hassan accepted that I came to stride with him on equal footing
And I would not stand in front of him
Nor walk behind him

> *With you, my fatigue left my body and soul*
> *Homesickness slowly died and I felt alive again*
> *With you, I reach the endless heights of womanhood*
> *The peaks of forgiveness and pride*
> *The peaks of pure feminine love*

Both of us . . .
Hand in hand
Through loving gazes
And with caring tones in our voices
Reassured one another that this is only a humane change for the better . . .
And no one is to be harmed by this new arrangement

> *With you, I am a fruitful tree*

With you, I am more than most
With you I am better than the best
With you I am something else

Let me tell you about the girls. (Pause)
It took two or three years for them to rediscover themselves
Sometimes I think . . .
We stole their childhood from them by our forced migration,
A childhood that could have been filled with comforts
And pleasures.
My kids didn't really have a childhood
They grew up too fast
However, they never blamed us for the path we chose.
Today they are both successful and happy
They appreciate the opportunities they have been given
And don't take the amenities of their host country for granted[6]
Amir and I have worked hard to create a better life
And a closer relationship
With every passing day
I am happier and happier that I am here

I have arrived with empty hands
I have come from a distant land
With hope in my heart
I came looking for the light

At first,
My happiness was for the girls,
BUT now
I am happy for myself, too. (Smile)
You know . . .
Even though it took a long time for me to discover the identity I had lost
    to my unwanted migration,
As a human being,
I now have a broader perspective on life and myself.

I filled my backpack with life's experiences
And through it all, lost my childhood memories
Memories of grandmother's Jasmine perfume and fine thread
Her fairy tales and the scent of bread

Basically
I feel that I have gained opportunities that otherwise I could never have
    achieved
Had I not decided to emigrate.

Through thick and thin
I've seen it all without and within

Dreams of freedom I once had in my motherland
Came true on my journey to a faraway land

NOTES

1. Masoud Sepand, "Havaye Khaneh" (A feeling of home), (n.d.) http://massoudse-pand.blogspot.com (last accessed October 26, 2019).

2. Sepand, "Havaye Khaneh."

3. Sepand, "Havaye Khaneh."

4. Sepand, "Havaye Khaneh."

5. Nasrin is referring to a playlet within Bertolt Brecht's (1938) *Fear and Misery of the Third Reich*, trans. John Willett (London: Bloomsbury Methuen Drama, 2009; repr. 2015).

6. This concept is more fully developed in Benjamin Giguère, Richard N. Lalonde, and Evelina Lou's essay, "Living at the Crossroads of Cultural Worlds: The Experience of Normative Conflicts by Second Generation Immigrant Youth," showing that most second-generation immigrants become bi-cultural, feeling comfortable switching between the two languages of origin and the host county; feeling comfortable in either culture (*Social and Personality Psychology Compass* 4, no. 1 [2010]: 14–29, http://dx.doi.org/10.1111/j.1751-9004.2009.00228.x).

Six

A Girl with an American Husband

Shahla

(Setting: An old suitcase with a shawl over it in the middle of stage. A high stool, guitar on a guitar stand. Ziba picks up the shawl, wraps it around her shoulder and sits on the high stool.)

I was twenty-two when I met Tim in Iran
We were both working in an American company.
We were going out together for a couple of months
Until the Americans were forced to leave Iran
Tim went back to America.
We wanted to get married
But not that quickly! (Smile)
The Islamic Revolution rushed us into marriage
Therefore, I left Iran for England in 1979
And we got married in there

> *Sky is bluer than yesterday*
> *My day is better than yesterday*
> *The one I prayed for*
> *Finally became mine today*

Everything was as good as I had dreamed of (Content voice)
For the first five or six years
We were traveling due to Tim's line of work
We were living an American life
Our home environment
The air we breathed
The music we listened to
The language we spoke
Annnny noise that we heard

Even my thoughts were American![1]
Little by little
I got tired of traveling and moving from one place to another
I wanted a permanent home
I wanted permanent friends and a stable social life.
So, like many we chose the sunny Los Angeles, California (Smile)
By moving to Los Angeles, our one-hundred-percent American lifestyle
     started to change
And it slowly tilted towards a Persian lifestyle (A half smile)

> *A new day, a new destiny*
> *A breath of fresh air*

Soon, we were surrounded by Iranian friends who although could all
     speak English (Pause)
Spoke in Persian!
Tim didn't mix with Iranians
And his conversation rarely went beyond casual greetings.
Following the Persian socializing
Was Iranian grocery shopping
Persian food,
And Persian restaurant-going
AND to top it all off,
The one-hour of Persian TV shows on Sunday
Which I anxiously waited for[2] (Pause)
I remember on one of those Sundays
I was home alone
Watching my favorite Persian program
And Moein our famous male singer, was singing:

> *I wish to go back to Isfahan (a city in Iran)*
> *Once again see that beautiful city.*
> —Moein (lyrics by Sheybani)[3]

I was really enjoying the song
Until Tim entered the room and tried to imitate the singer
Shouting *"Yai! Yai! Yai! Yai!"* (Loud voice)
I am sure he didn't mean to make fun of my culture[4]
Or insult or hurt me
But the music sounded strange to him
And he was not at fault.
Later on I could even justify it,
Thinking that this is how I would react if someone takes me to a Native
     American village and asks me to listen to native music!
One always must be fair. (Three-second pause)
Tim tried hard at the beginning to learn Persian

He took a Persian language class at UCLA.
I remember the night when he came home from his class
And to show me how much he learned he said:

"*Chetori Zaifeh?*" ("How'dy weak woman"?)

I replied

"What did you say?" (Wondering voice)

He repeated and explained that his teacher told him in Persian they call
women "weak"! (Pause)
I told him
"Your teacher is illiterate and doesn't know anything about Persian language and Persian culture." (Angry voice)

The word "*Zaifeh*" is used to insult a woman
And it is not a kind of word you should learn (Pause)
That was the last Persian class he took!
And after that Tim never showed interest in learning Persian (Three-
second pause)
Later, he started getting back pain
To the point that he couldn't move and lost his job
Though, culturally, I was brought up to be someone's wife (Incredulous
voice)
And never thought of being the bread earner
I had no choice but to look for a job
And reluctantly start working. (Three-second Pause)
For years, I thought I was doing Tim a favor
I thought that he was responsible for the two of us
And I was just helping him for the moment (Pause)
Living in America with Tim
Allowed me to taste the real flavor of equality between men and women
Life is full of surprises! (Soft Smile and pause)
In the Persian community, I was known as "The girl with American
husband"
No one bothered to learn my name
They just referred to me as "the girl with American husband!" (Pause)
When I met someone the first question was:

"How is life with an American husband?"
"How come you married an American?" (Three-second pause)

Once I met an Iranian lady divorcing her American husband
Complaining of how she got tired of hearing

"I love you" instead of "*Dooset daram,*"

She said

"I want to come home and have him say *"Salam"* instead of "Hi"
"Chi mikhori?" instead of "What would you like to eat?"

And so on . . . (Doubtful look and pause)
It took me some time to really understand what she was really talking
   about! (Three-second pause)
In the parties when people wanted to praise me, they said

"Our beautiful Persian girls are taken by American men"

Or

"Where were you when my son was looking for a Persian girl?"

Slowly people's comments started to affect me
I gave too much attention and credit to some of them
And took some of them too seriously
To the point that I began to think
"What if?"
What if, he called me *"Azizam"*, instead of "Honey"?
What if, when coming home he shouted *"Kojaee?"* instead of *"Where are
   you?"*
What if he said *"Dasted dard nakoneh"* instead of "Thank you"?[5]
AND . . . Many, many more *"What ifs"*
Slowly *"What ifs"* turned into *"I wish"* (Three-second pause)
It was then that I took a closer look at my life and realized: (Romantic
   tune)

> *It is about the time we have been together*
> *It is about our laughter through tough times*
> *If one takes a good look into the past*
> *We really don't have many bad memories*
> *It has been a long time that wherever I go, your thought is with me*
> *Your love is the most beautiful chapter of my life*

I took a closer look at the people around me
And noticed there are many that, though they speak my language
Don't have anything in common with me
Though we are coming from the same culture and country
We are so different from one another
It's as if we are coming from two different universes (Pause)
I took a closer look at my relationship with Tim
And noticed the amount of respect
Trust
And understanding between us
These are the most important things in life. (Pause)

I appreciate his peacefulness
His love
His smile when encountering life's turbulences
His comforting words telling me

"Don't worry, I will take care of it." (Three-second pause)

After years
I re-evaluated myself and my life
I wanted to find out for myself why I married an American man.
I noticed at the age of twenty-two, that I made the right choice (Convincing voice)
Without even knowing it! (Smile)
I realized that the relationship between two people has nothing to do with their culture
Religion
Language
Or the color of their skin
People's relationships only depend on their humanness,
Their beliefs, and their values.
Yes, I made a right decision when I was twenty-two
Our humanness is what makes life beautiful (Smile, happy tune)

> *The ceiling is made with kindness*
> *The floor is made with love*
> *The walls are made with kindness*
> *The windows are made with trueness and honesty*
> *Our home is a golden castle, far from bad omen*
> *You and I are the best lovers,*
> *You are the one I wished for*

NOTES

1. For more on the development of host communication competence in relationship to an individual's capabilities pertaining to communicative engagement with the host environment see Young Yun Kim's "Intercultural Personhood: Globalization and a Way of Being," *International Journal of Intercultural Relations* 32, no. 4 (2008): 359–68, http://dx.doi.org/10.1016/j.ijintrel.2008.04.005.

2. Hamid Naficy believes Iranian exilic television shaped many lives. "reflecting the formlessness of liminality, it first emerges as a hermetically sealed collection of audiovisuals put together with great individual effort by producers and addressed to what was thought to be a homogeneous audience (*The Making of Exile Cultures: Iranian Television in Los Angeles* [Minneapolis: University of Minnesota Press, 1993], 124). See further discussion of Naficy, *Making of Exile Cultures*, chap. 1.

3. Jamshid Sheybani, "Delam mikhad be Esfahan bargardam" (I wish I could return to Isfahan), sung by Moein (1990), https://pikdo.net/p/ostad_moein_saeed/208362568356185504 9_6087221823 (accessed October 26, 2019).

4. Kenneth Burke believes language is action loaded with emotion. Therefore, no word can be neutral. See Burke's *The Philosophy of Literary Form* (Berkeley: University of California Press, 1974).

5. She was not aware of the effect that people's interaction had on her behavior in regards to her marriage. In "Self-Shock: The Double-Binding Challenge of Identity," Rhonda Zaharna explains the link between self, others and behavior. "We may not be aware of how our own self-images reflect others' images of us because," as Vallacher noted, "we internalize—adopt as our own—the perspectives of others" (*International Journal of Intercultural Relations* 13, no. 4 [1989]: 506, https://doi.org/10.1016/0147-1767(89)90026-6).

Seven

Made in America, Delivered in Iran

Shahrzad Safinya

(Setting: An old suitcase with a shawl over it in the middle of stage. A high stool, guitar on a guitar stand. Ziba picks up the shawl, wraps it around her shoulder and sits on the high stool.)

> *Sometimes I am hidden and sometimes revealed*
> *Sometimes I am a Muslim, a Christian or a Jew*
> *To fit my heart into everyone else's heart*
> *Each day I am someone other and new*
> —Rumi [1]

My father was studying in New York and working at the United Nations after World War II

My parents were in love with one another since childhood

They got married and my mother came to the United States with an army airplane

Both of my brothers and my sister were born in America

I am the last child

As my father used to say, I was "made in America, delivered in Iran!" (Smile)

When I was born my father passed an entrance examination and was hired in the Ministry of Foreign Affairs

In a way, I was my father's calendar; whenever he wanted to see how long he had been working at Ministry of Foreign Affairs, he would refer to me. . . .

> *When I was born, the calendar was born*
> *My father's Shahrzad, the storyteller, was born*
> *I became his one and only*
> *Let me tell you my story*

73

I was two years old when I first left Iran with my family
My father was transferred to Prague as a Consul General
And we stayed there for three years
In fact, my first words were in Czech
Perhaps because my nanny was Czechoslovakian!
My parents didn't understand me then! (Smile and pause)
We were constantly moving because of my father's job
Four years in each country.
We moved to London and lived there for four years
I spoke English
We moved to Ankara and lived there for four years
I spoke Turkish
And I spoke Chinese when we moved to Beijing for four years!
Wherever we lived I could speak the language
BUT my facial features and appearance never matched the language I
    spoke
I never had the right facial features
Wherever I went I was asked

> *Tell me where you are coming from*
> *Which land do you belong to, which city, which town?*
> *In this strange land you look familiar, friendly*
> *Which land are you coming from, which city, which town?*
> *Tell me where you are coming from*

All these years I was living in fear of my father coming home, telling us
    that it was time to pack and move to another country
And my mother who stood by him like a mountain would calmly pack our
    suitcases
AND I would never again see the people that I made friends with
Or my teachers
Or the ice-cream man
I was tired of moving and relocating every four years (Pause)
In between each move we came to Iran and stayed for a short while
If school were in session
I would go to the school that was owned by my uncle
So that I wouldn't fall behind on my education
If it happened to be summer
I would just enjoy spending time with friends and family
I was fifteen or sixteen years old when my father asked the Ministry of
    Foreign Affairs not to be sent out of the country for a while
This was so that I could spend time in Iran and graduate from high school
My sister and two brothers were studying in university in the United
    States

While I registered for high school in Iran
In less than six months
My father came home and said
It is time to pack . . .
We are leaving for America
So, we moved to San Francisco in November of 1974
(Three-second pause)
A week after we celebrated my sixteenth birthday.
We lived in San Francisco for two years
I had just graduated from high school when my father came home and
    said
It is time to pack
We are leaving for another country
This time I stayed in San Francisco and my parents moved to Jakarta
    (Pause)
I decided to study photography in college
I made new friends
And felt safe knowing that I didn't have to move to another country
    anymore.
The college encouraged students to travel to any place in the world and
    take pictures for school credit
I decided to travel to Jakarta
To see my parents and take pictures there as well.
It was January 1979 (Low voice)
The revolution in Iran had just started
Every day there was something in the news about Iran
I could see the worriedness in my father's eyes
He didn't talk much
None of us talked much
Our home environment had changed
Everybody was quiet, as if no one had anything to say
My father knew there were major changes about to happen
BUT never in his wildest dreams did he think that it would end how it
    did!
I remember that day
January 16th, 1979
My father came home and said,
"The worst has happened. His majesty left Iran!"
(Loud voice and powerful tune)

> One person had left the country but
> Many lives had been affected
> One book had been closed but
> Many stories just began

It was a horrifying time
Our environment was filled with a kind of uncertainty and worry
For two days no one talked
We communicated through
Tears
Silence
And mournful glances
I was supposed to come back by the end of January to start school again
BUT I couldn't leave my parents in that situation
I called the school
And came back to America at the end of February
Immediately applied for a job at immigration
And got hired as a translator
I was on-call
I was mostly in contact with Iranians who left the country for different
    reasons
I liked my job, but I was saddened to hear stories of Iranian immigrants
    who had lost everything and were now dependent on one person's
    decision
A judge once told me
"You are a true translator; Iranians cry in Farsi and you translate their
    cries into English."

We cried all night long, we cried till dawn, we cried every step of the migration journey
When they were cutting the trees, we cried hearing each striking sound of the axe
                                                                —Qahaar Assi[2]

Iran's government mandated that all the Consuls to go back to Iran
In fact, Iran's government asked every country not to grant visa to any
    Consuls
So, they had no choice but to go back to Iran.
My father wanted to return to Iran
He kept saying
"I did nothing but give genuine and honest service to my country and to
    my people; why should I worry? No one would harm me. I will go
    back to Iran."
My mother agreed with everything that my father said
She said
"just because the government had changed, it doesn't mean that his ser-
    vices to Iran would be ignored, we would go back to Iran (Pause)
It was as if they were living in a dream
As if they couldn't see or hear about their friends who were being impris-
    oned or executed one after another
My father had many friends in various consulates

BUT no one could help him (Loud voice and powerful tune)

> *One person had left the country, but*
> *Many lives had been affected*
> *One book had been closed, but*
> *Many stories just began*

My siblings and I were desperately looking to find a way to bring our
  parents to America
Finally, with the help of an American judge, we were able to get a Green
  Card for my parents
This was based on the fact that, three of their children were born in and
  lived in America and by law, their residency could not be denied
Luckily their file moved forward quickly, and they came to America
However, we were worried about my father's safety
Because many of his friends had been assassinated by Islamic agents
  around the world. (Three-second pause)
My parents lived in a small cabin in the San Francisco Bay Area for over
  two years
My father was restless
But my mother kept her usual smile and didn't allow fear to take over the
  love between us
My father used to say: All that we have is because of your mother

> *Whatever we have is because of you*
> *We are incomplete without you*
> *May you always protect us*
> *With you, we have nothing to worry about*

We went to the cabin for visits on Saturdays
We would stay a night and come back Sunday afternoon to go to work on
  Monday
It was not easy for my father to live in hiding
He was frustrated
He said,
"I have lost everything and if I cannot be close to my kids, this life will be
  worthless."
It was a tough time for all of us
After two years my father came out of hiding, and life got better

> *Rainy days left our home*
> *Sun shined through the windows*
> *My father became lively*
> *Sadness had left him*

Like many other Iranians we had to leave everything in Iran
We lost all we had

But my father didn't care about material things
He used to say,

"When you are driving a car, the front window is vast"

Because you need to give your full attention to the front
But the rearview mirror is small
Because the past is not as important as the future

> *Passed times would never come back again*
> *There is an ongoing story of life*
> *That never again can start from the beginning*

Fortunately, I could concentrate on the front mirror and start a new life
    (Pause)
I always had a passion for baking
So I found a job in a French pastry shop in Los Angeles and learned how
    to bake
I also worked as a photographer on weekends and evenings
Going to weddings and bat mitzvahs taking pictures
After eight months living in Los Angeles I went back to Northern Califor-
    nia and opened my own pastry shop in Oakland
I worked eighteen hours a day
Distributing my pastries to café's, hotels and restaurants
It was in Oakland where I met Saeed my husband
He became a good friend of mine first and then he became my husband
    (Smile)
Although if you ask him, he says

"I reached for his hand the first time we met!"

But, that's all right
He is the best thing that ever happened in my life

> *You don't have to say "I love you"*
> *I'll say it. "I love you"*
> *I know what to look for in your eyes*
> *But once in a while, it would be nice to look in my eyes*
> *Call me by my name and tell me "I love you"*

I sold the bakery after marriage
But continued working in an immigration office as a translator
Soon after I was blessed with two baby twin girls
And a son the year after
Though I was too busy with the kids and pursuing job opportunities,
I started voluntarily helping with Iranian cultural events.
I still do . . .
I sell tickets in Iranian film festivals and help them with translation.

I do as much as I can.

My involvement with Iranian cultural organizations keeps me lively and energizes me.

Sometimes it is upsetting to me to see my Iranian friends raising American flags on top of their roofs and celebrating every non-Iranian custom,

But not embracing Persian traditions,

Including Nowruz, the Persian New Year

> *Sometimes I am happy with my memories*
> *Sometimes I am happy to hear Iran's national anthem*
> *Sometimes though, I can't take it anymore*
> *I want to scream, I want to shout*

Though I never lived in Iran for an extended period
There isn't a day that passes where I don't think about Iran
My father taught us to be proud of our Persian heritage
And of being Iranian
He used to tell us,

"No matter how well educated you'll be
No matter how many other languages you speak
If you cannot read the signs in your own country
You will be considered illiterate."

My mother has her own rules, though she is fluent in English
She doesn't allow her children and grandchildren to speak to her in any language other than Farsi
As simple as that! (Pause)
Let me give you an example that illustrates the importance of reading and writing Farsi in our home
When my brother, Kambiz, was studying physics at Harvard University in the sixties
He had to write to my parents in Farsi
It took a minimum of three weeks for his letter to come from the U.S. to Beijing
God forbid if my mother noticed a misspelled word!
Right away, she would make a correction and send it back to Kambiz
My poor brother had to write the corrected word twenty times and send it back to my mother
To make sure that he knew how to read and write Farsi correctly
This process took almost six weeks! (Smile)
This is a family joke now! (Pause)
I always speak Farsi with my kids

Whenever they spoke English to me in their early years, I just looked at
    them
Acting like I didn't understand a word of what they were saying!
When my son was two and half years old
He asked me, in English,

"What is *hospital* in Farsi?"

Right away I replied, in Farsi

"Bimarestaan"

He looked at me and said,

"Gotcha!"

I didn't respond![3] (Smile and pause)
I do admit that I took them to Farsi classes by force
But now they appreciate it and they are happy and grateful for speaking
    another language
All three of them are now able to read and write in Farsi

> *" F" as in freedom that cost us our lives*
> *" M" as in mother, the kindest, strongest*
> *" P" as in patience, needed to survive*
> *" H" as in heart, which was broken through the years*

I wanted my children not to feel any difference between them and the
    non-Iranians.
So, I put up a large Christmas tree at home and we all decorated it
    together.
We had the most elaborate Christmas decorations in the neighborhood.
But I also made sure that my children knew about Nowruz
The Persian New Year
I still make sure that they are familiar with Persian culture and that they
    respect their heritage (Pause)
One day, my father was with me while I was baking in the kitchen
My son, Cyrus, was thirteen years old then
The bell rang
I opened the door
A thirteen-year-old American boy walked in
Looked at me and without saying a word of greeting walked to my son's
    room
I came back to the kitchen and continued baking (Upset voice)
BUT I couldn't let it go of that attitude
I went to Cyrus's room and knocked on his door
He opened the door and asked if I need anything

Yes honey there is a problem!
What is it mom?
I am sorry to say that when I told you that you are no different from non-Iranians
I was wrong! (Serious tone)
You are different!
We are different.
I hope you would never go to someone's home without greeting his or her parents and the elderly.
Your grandfather and I are respectable human beings! (Pause)
I give you two choices
One is for you to ask your friend
To leave our home
Ring the bell
And come in as if he is just meeting us for the first time
While respectfully greeting us
OR two
I will ask him how to respect the rules and culture of this family (Pause)
Cyrus responded No, no, mom . . . I will ask him

When I came back to the kitchen my father asked,

"What happened? What did you tell Cyrus?"
"Nothing" I said

My father continued,
"He is just a teenager, don't badger him."
"Teaching your kids to be polite and say hello when walking into someone's home is not badgering or bothering."
You taught us too
Why is it that everybody thinks this is badgering? (A bit angry tone)
This is being polite
It doesn't make sense to walk into someone's home and disrespect the people living in that home! (Three-second pause)
A couple of minutes later
My son's friend walked out and rang the bell
I opened the door
He walked in with smile and said

"Hi Mom, how are you?"

I kindly replied
Hi sweetheart, I am fine, how are you?
He walked to my father
Hugged him and said
Hi grandpa, how are you doing?"
My father responded with kindness
And he went to Cyrus's room
We could hear them laughing for an hour (Three-second pause)

That boy is twenty-five-years old not
To this day, whenever he sees me, he hugs me and tells me, "You taught
    me something that I never would otherwise have learned!

> *It is good to greet people with a smile*
> *It is an opportunity to meet new people*
> *A Simple greeting , sincere kind words*
> *May bring a long-life friendship into your life*

I have travelled to Iran a couple of times
Honestly, the first time I didn't feel welcomed
Especially when the kids were young.
It was not easy to find their necessities
Simple things like diapers and milk (Pause)
The first time we all went for a walk in our old neighborhood
My son was in a stroller and the twins were old enough to walk
Suddenly my daughter asked,

"Mom, why are the streets broken?"

She was right (Sad low voice)
She described it perfectly with her childish tongue
I felt the same
Everywhere looked gray
As if Tehran were covered with sadness and misery

> *Everywhere was familiar but I couldn't recognize any place*
> *I roamed everywhere*
> *Everything was new,*
> *While I was looking for the past*
> *There are high-rises instead of old arboretums*
> *The gray color of the city is heartbreaking*

Later on
I felt more welcomed
Or perhaps I got used to it! (Half smile- pause)
It was on one of my trips to Iran when I got into a cab and started to talk
    to the driver
He asked me where I was coming from

"Iran, I am Iranian"
"I mean where is your country of origin?"
"I was born in Iran"
"But you are not Iranian!"
"What makes me not Iranian?"

"You don't walk like Iranian women; you don't interact like an Iranian
woman! You don't even talk like Iranian women! I don't know where
you are coming from; but wherever it is, stay as you are."

I told him that I have been away from Iran for years, but I love my
country

When I got out of the cab

I walked up and down the street crying

I cried hard (Sad/low voice)

I cried because all my life wherever I went

I was asked, "Where are you coming from?"

I cried because my own countryman didn't count me as one of his own
and asked me where I came from

I cried because for years whenever I said my name

No one asked me *Who*?

They asked *What?*

I cried because I was tired of telling and explaining to everybody how to
pronounce my name

My name is Shahrzad. . . . No, no, *not* Sha-her-zad. It's Shahr-zad!

> *The name that had been with me all my life*
> *The name that shares my happiness and sorrow*
> *The name that reminds me of ME*
> *Sometimes brings tears into my eyes*

Whenever I am about to make a trip to Iran, I tell my American friends
that I am going back home

A friend of mine once said, "Shahrzad, America is your home; you have
spent most of your lifetime in this country."

I told her that, if I had a choice, I wouldn't choose America as my home

> *I am from the desolated land of Iran*
> *One day, I will go back*
> *I won't stay here forever*
> *Though the host country had been kind to me*
> *I am happy that I am only a guest here*

My kids love Iran, too, all three of them asked to be sent to Iran as their
graduation gift

We have travelled every corner of that country together, Shiraz, Esfahan,
Mashhad, Bam, Kashan.

> *My homeland smells like rosewater*
> *Its aroma is better than musk and ember*
> *Its soil smells like heaven in all seasons*
> *As if winter is making love with spring*

You know what?

That government has nothing do to with me. (Angry and sad low voice)

I have nothing to do with Ahmadinejad or Khomenei.
BUT Iran is my country,
Iran is my home.
I don't like to think that it will never become as glorious as it was before.

> *There was a time when my land was glorious*
> *It was far from bad and evil*
> *That beautiful land of Iran*
> *Was like a peerless gem*

If the government changes and Iran become a democratic country, I
   would like to go back to live in Iran
Even though I have not lived there for many years (Pause)
All my life I adjusted myself with people of different cultures and races
Why shouldn't I be able to adjust myself with the people of my own
   country?

> *That land, whether flourishing or desolate,*
> *It is my homeland, it is Iran*

Yes, If Iran ever changes to a democratic country
I would like to go back and live with my countrymen and women and
   adjust myself to the people who speak my language

> *That land, whether flourishing or desolate,*
> *It is my homeland, it is Iran*

NOTES

1. This poem is attributed to Rumi, the mystic thirteenth-century poet. There are no extant Persian verses of this available.

2. Qahaar Assi, "Geristim" (We cried), (1989), http://qahaar-assi.blogfa.com/1386/06 (last accessed on October 26, 2019).

3. Having three children born in America, Shahrzad had to get involved with the new culture while maintaining and practicing the culture of her origin. See my discussion of John Berry's stages of different responses to acculturation and assimilation in the introduction-. Also see Stella Ting-Toomey's work *Communicating Across Cultures* (New York: Guilford Press, 1999) on how individuals develop a sense of identity and acquire meanings, values, norms, and styles of communication through daily interactions with others.

Eight

Unfulfilled Dreams

Shervin

(Setting: An old suitcase with a shawl over it in the middle of stage. A coatrack with a man's shirt hanging on one of the racks. Ziba sits on the chair and says: "I don't know how many of you have ever heard of the French actor, Alain Delon? He was sort of the George Clooney of the 70's; the single reason for success of many French movies. I know of someone who wanted to be an actor after he saw Alain Delon's movie at the age of thirteen and I want to share his story with you." Ziba cues the technician to play the song with Alain Delon's voice "Paroles Paroles" Dalida et Alein Delon. A picture of Alain Delon is projecting on the screen. While music is playing, Ziba walks into the audience section and borrows a gentleman's tie, and calmly returns to the stage as the character; points at the picture and says:)

> Yes . . . that is him. I was thirteen when I first saw his movie; I wanted to be an actor ever since . . . (Music Ends)
> I am tired of moving from one place to another
> We have been migrating since I was a kid
> I was twelve when we left Mazandaran's mountains to small town of Saari and then to Tehran
> The capital city
> Because my older brother was accepted in the university of Tehran (Pause)
> Tehran was not a pleasant experience for me
> It was a strange encounter with a society I had heard from afar
> New people
> With new sets of mentality (Three-second pause)
> It took me some time to find my way around
> Sometimes by fighting

And sometimes by friendship (Pause)

I was about to be fourteen when my father died

And my brother and I continued living in Tehran under my mother's supervision

My mother was in love with Persian and French literature (Music playing Low Volume "La Mamma" Charles Aznavour on background)

Every once in a while, she used melodic French words in her daily conversation

To encourage us to learn French. (Pause)

I was about to graduate from the University

When suddenly my mom passed away . . . (Head down thinking, music playing high volume for ten-second and ends, head up)

And I left Iran in the winter of 1972 to continue my education in France.

Soon I became accustomed to Paris

Continued my education

And got married. (Pause)

The Iranian revolution had already started

When I received my doctorate in archeology as well as urban design and architecture in 1978 in France.

My sister-in-law invited us to Ohio

And we stayed with them for two months (Pause)

Though my brother told us

"No one with a right mind would come to Iran in this situation."

We did just that!

And four months before Ayatollah Khomeini's victorious return to Iran

I came back to Iran with my wife

And started working in the northern part of Iran

Because I always wished to be productive in my own place of birth

I wanted to be a part of its economic and social development

Alas the workplace was closed due to strikes

And my dreams were shattered . . . (Sad voice)

Though I was not in good terms with the Shah and his monarchy

I was not for revolution either

Especially the Islamic type!

Five or six months later

I went back to Paris and my pregnant wife went to her sister's in America

(Music playing low volume "Emmenez Moi" Charles Aznavour on background)

I joined a Political group in France and fought against the Islamic Republic,

Every morning I had a meeting with the heads of different opposition groups

And every afternoon we changed regimes in coffee houses!

We had such big ideas!

The battle was much longer than what I expected (A half smile, thinking, high volume music plays for ten-second and ends)

I asked my wife to come back to Paris.

Our first child and, two years later, our second child were born in Paris

After four years of ineffective political battles against the Islamic Republic of Iran,

We moved to America in hopes of a better life

Perhaps our biggest mistake was to choose Los Angeles as our new home (Three-second pause)

I started pointless political involvements

And going to Persian parties and gatherings along with my wife

Conversations mostly started with the same stupid question of

"How is your Business?"

And finished with inconclusive arguments between the people who personally advised and warned His Majesty Shah of Iran of an upcoming revolution! (Pause)

Living in Los Angeles

There was no need to learn English

Even when we dialed the wrong number

Someone replied in Persia: *agha avazi gerefti*, "Sir, you got the wrong number!"

Everywhere we went there was a compatriot who understood our language and took care of us . . .

Whether we were in need of a mechanic to fix our car

OR a doctor to fix our body

In fact, I learned my English from my fellow countrymen who used many English words within their Persian conversations! (Soft smile)

Yet I had problems understanding the non-Iranians

I could only understand a few words [1] (Pause)

I remember once I was looking for a parking space in Westwood

As usual I made five or six unsuccessful rounds

Suddenly I saw an empty space

I saw a car ready to back up to the space

I cut in front of her with no hesitation and quickly parked my car

I was proud of my parking skills! (proud look)

The lady backed off

Pulled down the window

And started saying something in English

I didn't understand what she was saying

But in the middle of her screaming I heard her saying

"Go back to Iran"

As soon as I heard this
I got so angry and shouted back:

"Me go back to Iran? No, you go back to Iran!"

She shook her head and left
AND right then I thought to myself what a stupid reply!!!! (Shaking head)
Slowly we got used to living in Los Angeles,
To the point that we invited my sister-in-law and her husband from Ohio
    to come and live in this city that in many ways was like Iran
To ease the pain of migration (Pause)
My wife was able to find a job easily in the fashion industry
But I was still dreaming to find a job as an architect
Till a friend suggested opening a Limousine company
He said you can make a good living
Especially now that the Olympic Games are coming to LA.
I purchased a Cadillac with my brother-in-law
Added the needed parts
And we became Limousine drivers and owners
It was an easy job
And we were making good money
But I was constantly thinking about finding my way back to my own
    field.
There were no ancient buildings in Los Angeles to restore
BUT I was hoping to find a job in the field of architecture
Which has always been my passion.
I took advantage of every opportunity to find a job related to the architec-
    tural field
I worked with an American architect for a short while
In order to forget the French metric system
And learn inch and foot
And get some experience.
In those days pagers were new
Sometimes I took the Limousine by the job site
I was Mr. Architect
'Til the pager went off
And I became the driver to go pick up a client.
I met many people
In fact, my notion of American people came from driving the Limousine.
Sometimes I picked up famous stars

Once, I picked up Pierce Brosnan (Music Playing "James Bond Dr. NO theme tune" Fade up five seconds, then fade down, stays on background)

As soon as he sat down

I said Mr. Bond

I didn't even call him James

So, he wouldn't think I want to get too friendly with him!

He replied with anger:

"My name is Pierce Brosnan but seems like no one wants to learn!"

From then on, I never called any star by his original name

OR by his movie character name (Three-second pause, music ends)

Time went by

And my language difficulties were still with me

I converted every English word that I heard to French

Trying to find its meaning,

Meanwhile I believed the limousine customers could be the best clients for my architectural work

Because they have the money

And if they only knew what a great architect I am

There is a chance to find a job . . .

So, I took advantage of every situation to tell my clients about myself and my education.

One night I picked up a young man from Beverly Hills.

Per his request

I picked up a young girl from another place and drove them to Malibu under the moonlight (Music playing "La Nuit" Salvatore Adamo, six-second high volume and then stays background as low volume.)

As I was driving

They got sexually involved.

To give them privacy

I rolled up the privacy divider between us.

Every now and then

The young man pulled down the privacy divider

Asked me a question

Started sexual interaction with the girl

And I rolled it up again.

After a while he pulled down the divider and asked me to take him to disco, *oh la la.*

A minute before reaching there

He shouted: do you want a *blue job*? (Calm voice)

Since I had noticed

Everything in America has a connection to colors

Like *green card* for residency
Pink slip for car ownership
Yellow page for telephone book
And it is obvious to everybody that, *blue* is the color of royals and monarchy
I thought to myself *thank God*
Somebody noticed what I should really be doing
And is offering me a very high-class job! (Pause)
To show him who I really am; I proudly replied:

> *Oh, yes sir, I am very interested* (Heavy Persian Accent)
> *Actually, I have my PhD in architecture and urban planning!*

He looked at me in a strange way thinking why one would need a PhD for this job???!!! (Shaking head)
He got off the car and left me alone with the young girl
And came back after half an hour
Mumbling something which as usual I didn't understand and just smiled.
He had a short conversation with the girl
Shook his head and told me to take them back,
(Music ends after three-second)
The next day I went to the office and told my partner
Make sure you give me the phone number of the young man I picked up last night
I think he has a good job for me!
My partner asked
What kind of Job?
I replied
He didn't say much he just said it is a *blue job*!!!
I heard everybody laughing
They explained the true meaning to me
And I left the office with sorrow of not knowing the language . . .
And no, I did not get that job! (Smile and pause)
Nevertheless, without knowing the English language
Our Limousines added up
I opened my architecture office
And although the Limousine Company was making good money
I sold my share and continued to work as an architect
Though I must admit
The money I was making as a Limousine driver was way more!
(Three-second pause)
To be honest
I never felt comfortable in this system and life
My life abroad spent itself in hopeful dreams . . .

Unfulfilled . . .
I always felt everything is temporary here
And there is a place that
IF I get there
Everything will be permanent (Music playing "Yesterday When I Was
    Young" Charles Aznavour, fade down, stays in background)
When I look back,
I see my life full of unfulfilled dreams . . .
As if everything is unfinished . . .[2]
Perhaps if I would have stayed in one place,
I would have known a smaller world and had a better ending.
Whether in Mazandaran's mountains,
Whether in Saari,
Whether in Tehran . . .
or in Paris . . . (Music fades up, Ziba takes off the tie, shirt and leaves the
    stage as music continues to play)

NOTES

1. Kalervo Oberg explains "Culture shock is precipitated by the anxiety that results from losing all our familiar signs and symbols of Social intercourse." He points to refusal of learning the new language of the host country and socializing with one's fellow countrymen as symptoms of culture shock (Oberg, "Cultural Shock: Adjustment to New Cultural Environments," *Curare* 7, no. 2 [1960]: 177–82; repr. *Curare* 29, no. 2 [2006]: 142, https://www.academia.edu/17206900/Cultural_Shock_Adjustment_to_new_cultural_environments_-_Kalervo_Oberg [accessed September 30, 2019]).

2. "The term 'Sojourner' has been used to describe between-society culture travelers . . . This label reflects the assumption that their stay is temporary, and that there is an intention to return to the culture of origin once the purpose of the visit has been achieved, assumptions which are often incorrect, as we shall see" (Colleen A. Ward, Stephen Bochner, and Adrian Furnham, *The Psychology of Culture Shock*, 2nd ed. [Philadelphia: Taylor & Francis, 2001], 6). Perhaps the thought of going back to his homeland would not allow him to move forward.

Nine

A Simple Dream

Valentina Nazaretian

(Setting: An old suitcase with a shawl over it in the middle of stage. A high stool, guitar on a guitar stand. Ziba picks up the shawl, wraps it around her shoulder and sits on the high stool.)

I was thirteen when the Islamic Republic came to power
Though I was covering my hair carefully
Every week I had run-ins with the Islamic forces
It was a time of anarchy
It was against the Islamic rule for boys and girls to socialize
And we were constantly arrested
But as soon as we were brought into the police station
The head officer would shout
Why did you bring them? (Loud voice)
Can't you see they are Armenian Christians?
Let them go (Careless voice)
It is all right in Christianity for men and women to socialize (Pause)
Five years had passed since the revolution
I got used to wearing a scarf
I didn't think about it anymore
It didn't bother me anymore[1]

> *I believed whatever they said*
> *I got used to its good and bad*
> *This is the good thing about being a child,*
> *Simple minded, far from hatred*

I was eighteen when I met Haik, my husband
It was my dream to walk with him hand in hand in the park
Without Islamic guards harassing us

My dream was as simple as that! (Soft smile)
I really didn't ask for much
I yearned for basic freedom
And an opportunity to continue my education
And that was it!
I would have been content (Pause)
Later on when I married Haik
We decided to leave Iran for America
In hopes of finding a better life
And to be able to continue our education
We paid $3,000 to a family friend to help us procure a visa to enter Holland
We left Iran in 1989.

> *My life-partner and I, along with our hopes and dreams,*
> *Left our childhood city*
> *I kept my childhood memories*
> *Close to my purity and innocence*

During our short stay in Holland
We realized that we had a long way to go
And that the road was going to be bumpy (Nodding head)
In order to obtain an American visa
We had to find a way to get to Germany
There was a simple YET ILLEGAL way of entering Germany through a little village that was half in Holland and half in Germany
Right by the border was a kiosk guarded by a German officer
Most days there was no guard standing there
And one could easily walk the border to enter Germany
BUT, on the days that the guard was there
One had to go back and try again another time!
Luckily, we entered Germany on our first try (Smile)
Immediately we went to a friend and left our baggage and passports with him
Because, if the police had found our passports
They would send us back to Iran (Three-second pause)
We presented ourselves to the police station
I was twenty-two, and Haik was twenty-three
The young interrogator reminded us of Gestapo agents that we had seen in the movies
He asked: (Cold voice)

> *Where are you from?"*
> *Iran.*
> *How did you get here?*

By car.
How long did it take?
Twenty hours.
Which route did you take?
We don't know!
(We have been told to reply, "We don't know" to most of the questions!)
How much money you have?
Nothing! (He put his hand in Haik's pocket and found $100!)
What is this?

We convinced him that we didn't know about the money
Until he finally let us go
And sent us to a refugee camp

> *The universe was now on our side*
> *We had gotten lucky*
> *Or, maybe it was my mother's prayer behind us*
> *That was following us step by step*

Most refugee camps consisted of a huge room with thirty some single
   beds
Refugees had to stay there for a minimum of four months
Until their cases were processed
Luckily, they placed us in a two-bedroom apartment (Happy voice)
That we shared with an Indian couple
Each couple had a bedroom and shared a kitchen
A bathroom . . . and a shower
They were good housemates
We lived together for three weeks
Until the government provided us with a one-bedroom apartment
And basic furniture

> *Our little home became a place of hope*
> *Full of dreams and love*
> *To tell you the truth, that little place*
> *Was like the White House to us*

The United States didn't accept political asylum
So, we applied for religious asylum
On the other hand
Germany didn't accept religious asylum
So, we applied for political asylum there (Pause)
Though Haik and I were never involved in political matters
I used my imagination and wrote a sad scenario involving politics to
   present to the German government
So that our case would be handled as a political matter
I wrote:
My husband Haik had once had a problem at work

And Islamic militia broke into our home forcefully
I was pregnant at the time
And terrified by the encounter
I aborted my child
And was under stress for months
I don't want to go back to Iran to be reminded of that experience
I have to say
All the government agencies knew about our fake stories and scenarios
    (Half smile)
All the stories were mostly the same
Some harsher than the others
Soon after we got settled in Germany (Pause)
Many of our friends and relatives left Iran for different social and political
    reasons and applied for asylum
I was helping as many as I could with their stories
Therefore, my scenario writing improved
I became known for the power of my imagination and writing skills
    between the refugees (Big smile)
BUT my best scenario was the one I wrote for my seventy-year-old IL-
    LITERATE grandmother and her friend (Smile)
I wrote:
These two elderly ladies opened their great library of political books to
    students to help them with their research and the study of politics
However . . . when the Islamic militia found out about it
They forced themselves into their home and set their library on fire
I don't know why or how (Wondering look)
BUT, out of all the scenarios I had written this one was picked up by a
    reporter!
The next day a reporter and a photographer came to my grandma's place
    for an interview
And, since they couldn't understand the language
My husband became their translator
He shamefully put some untrue stories together and told the reporter
    (Shameful gesture)
The next day my grandma's picture was in the newspaper
Sitting with her friend
Staring at the camera with a dumbfounded look in her eye
The headline read

    "Two revolutionary grandmas were attacked by Islamic militia for the
        crime of having a library!"

AND THAT became my finale for my story writing!

The pen was dancing through my fingers
I admit, my fingers are avid adventurers
I was making stories for a long time
I am still in awe of the power of my imagination

Let's return to Haik and me

Though I wrote the scenario

We would constantly change the dates and story to prolong the application process

Had Germany accepted our application for asylum

We would have lost the opportunity to come to America

The Germans were not accepting of us

In fact, living in Holland and Germany lowered our expectations for life abroad

It was a tough time

I felt the pain of alienation in the core of my being

Sadness left no stars in the sky for me
Send me some stars if you can
I am saddened by this year-round winter
Send me springtime

We stayed in Germany for eleven months

Until the United States granted us asylum (Happy face)

We entered America in 1990 with $1000 in our pockets

It was about the same time that America was going through a financial crisis

BUT we were too poor to even notice it! (Smile)

Though we were both living a good life in Iran and our family could help us

We decided not to accept any financial support and to make it on our own (Pause)

We rented a small apartment and filled it with our friends' unwanted furniture

My uncle got us a refrigerator on a credit card that we paid for monthly

But, there were blue skies as far as you could see
There was a breeze of freedom, as much as you could want
Though we have no way of going back
Our hearts were filled with hopes for a brighter future

We were both taking English classes in Iran and knew some English . . .

Right away we registered at college and started to work.

At the beginning we were taking the bus everywhere

BUT later on, we purchased a Datsun for $500!

It was a great car

We had it for two years

Haik even made money with it
Delivering Chinese food (Smile)
We were living a simple life
BUT we were happy
Every chance we got we went to the beach or the park and walked togeth-
  er hand in hand
Talking and planning our future
It was great
We had a great time

> *This is happiness to me*
> *You and me together, in love*
> *Made for one another*
> *This is happiness to me*

Over twenty years had passed since we immigrated.
As life got better and better,
We became more demanding and wanted more than just a simple walk
  around the park!
Nowadays we can afford to live well.
Financial crises affects us as well! (Smile)
BUT life is good
The only thing I miss is Iran's spring and Nowruz (Persian New Year).

> *I am saddened, send me spring, send me a souvenir from my childhood days*
> *Though it may trouble you, Send some patience for your little girl*
> —Manijeh Dartoumian[2]

At the end of the day we are happy and pleased about our immigration
Most importantly . . .
I achieved my simple wish
To walk in the parks, hand-in-hand with Haik and to continue my educa-
  tion.
The only thing I lost after the Islamic Revolution was my teenage years.
It was as if my youth had been lost irretrievably:
Wherever I search, I cannot find it.

NOTES

1. She was going through the process of acculturation in her homeland. Josiane F. Hamers and Michel H. A. Blanc, in *Bilinguality and Bilingualism*, 2nd ed. (Cambridge: Cambridge University Press, 2000), argue that: "Acculturation occurs when an individual experience changes of behaviors as a result of being in contact with other cultures" (205). Along with the process of acculturation, deculturation often occurs simultaneously. Deculturation refers to the process of unlearning and replacing the culture of origin.

2. Manijeh Dartoumian, "Delam gerefteh" (My heart is heavy), (n.d.), http://dartoo-mian.blogfa.com/1388/12/3 (accessed October 26, 2019).

Stories

Ten

A Dream of Hope

Mahvash Dareshi Gheytanchi Levi

We were not a pretentious family; We never lived beyond our means in order to boast and make others jealous, never two-faced appearance and essence were always one. However, the revolution stunk up the principles of our lives. Hypocrisy came to dominate everything ranging from our political and social views to our choice of clothing.

We had two kinds of everything
a domestic family version and
a public version.

With the coming of the Islamic Revolution, each morning I had to lecture my teenage daughter about the moral virtues of the Imam [Ayatollah Khomeini] and the benefits of the Islamic Revolution before sending her off to school, praying that she had paid no attention to the critical conversations the night before between my husband and me about the revolution.

My younger daughter [speaking with irony] had put our minds at ease, by cutting her hair short, dressing like a boy, and telling everyone she was a boy in order not to have to wear a headscarf.

Our lives were filled with fear and doubt
The heart trembled at hearing a footstep
Sometimes under the blue sky
It feared the gaze of every stranger

Before the 1979 Iranian Revolution, I used to design test questions for the high school senior year final exams for the central province and its suburbs. After the revolution, a cleric from the Islamic Council came to the school district and asked: "We have 20,000 teachers. Why is it that a Jew designs the high school senior year final exam questions?" The answer given to him was that this lady is very trustworthy. During the seven years in which she has been in charge, the questions have not been leaked and have not been sold. It was customary for those who designed test questions to sell them. This filled their pockets with money and their students' hearts with joy. Once again, that year, I designed the test questions.

A few months later, one day when I was sitting in my office, a typical Hezbollah-looking man entered my office leering at me. At that time, I was pregnant with my son. I felt my face turning pale but tried to maintain my composure. No sooner had he arrived than he started making accusations. He claimed that everything in sight was stolen from public funds—chairs, tables, window blinds, refrigerator, and copier. Thank God I had receipts and documentation for everything. After he carefully examined the paperwork and was convinced, he said: "I want to see the classrooms." He was desperately searching for a pretext to shut down the school and send me back to domestic life. When we got to the library, he looked at the books and saw a copy of the Qur'an. He said in an ironic tone, "I didn't know that Jewish kids read the Quran." I told him that during the hours when the Jewish students read the Torah, the Muslim children read the Quran and that we considered religious education very important and had an officially salaried Quran teacher. Suddenly, he was deflated. In a gentler tone, he said, "Next week, please come to the Ministry of Culture to have a meeting with the head of the Islamic Council as well. *Adieu* and may your newborn be healthy, and may its birth be auspicious."

> *He thought that my God is not a real God*
> *My prayers are not answered by his God*
> *If he could only see with the heart's eye*
> *He would have known that our hearts are united, not separated*

After he left, the school janitor, Murad, rushed in with a knife in his hand and said: "Madame, do you see this knife? I swear to the holy Quran that if he had tried to arrest you, I would have killed him."

I said (in my best managed tone not to sound ironic): "Murad, what are you talking about? This respectable gentleman meant no harm to me!!!"

Murad then continued, that while he was directing the man to my office, he told him that "although this lady is Jewish, she has helped us in every way." He told the man that four years ago when we wanted to build a mosque in Abhar [a small town in Zanjan province] she collected 5,000 Tumans donation from her colleagues. I did a lot of things like that; collected money for surgeries, weddings, wakes, celebrations for the circumcision of baby boys. Why not? If you do good deeds, you will receive good deeds.

O my heart, to be compassionate is important, to feel the pain of the helpless, is important
How long you live, is not important, how you live, is important

—Babak Rambakhsh[1]

To make the story short, the inspection that day took place without any bloodletting. The following week I went to the Ministry of Culture to see the head of the Islamic Council. My file was sitting in front of him and it was clear that he knew my past. He mumbled and said: "It is true that you are very experienced and honest, but the country has changed. In the Islamic Republic, it is better for the principal to be a Muslim and for you, a Jew, to be a teacher!"

It was as if someone had poured ice water over me. I felt insulted. After all my hard work for the school, increasing the student body from 250 to 1,500, I was now being eliminated for not being Muslim! I was always so proud of myself for participating in building my country. I wrote the "Test Preparation Guide" for the high school senior year final exams. I participated in writing science and math textbooks. I conducted much research on methods of education from other countries and selected the best for Iran. I received many letters of appreciation and certificates of recognition. Now all of that is being ignored because I am Jewish?!

The pens turned and they got the upper hand, the tables turned and they took over Iran
Using capricious motivations and excuses, Muslim and non-Muslim were imprisoned
—Hadi Khorsandi[2]

I resigned honorably and took a job at the Armenian School. It was a very sad experience. A young student jumped from the third floor to commit suicide, I tried to catch her as she fell. This is something that I'm sure her mother would have done if she were there. She fell over me, I was badly injured and suffered from nerve damage, I couldn't hear anything for a long time.

The Iran-Iraq War was also affecting my depressed mood. One day, I took some pastry to visit the war disabled hospital that had over a thousand beds. One of the disabled patients who might have thought that I was a nurse called me and said, "I want to ask you a question, promise to tell me the truth. Now that I have lost a leg in the war, do you think people and society will accept me?" I felt terrible and said: "Of course they will, and with open arms. The people of Iran have not changed. Wait until the war ends and you will see how you will be honored by people."

When I came home, I broke down in tears. My husband said, "Don't you have enough sadness of your own to go visit the disabled? Why don't you go to the maternity ward or some place that would make you happy?" Those were strange times.

Sorrow and pain are not apart from us
Destiny is not in our hands
I tell myself: be patient
There is no alternative but to pray

You know, I liked living in Iran. Our neighborhood had Zoroastrians, Jews, Muslims, Bahai's. . . . Our kids were friends with each other, they played together. Mothers watched each other's kids. It was a good neighborhood, full of security and kindness. The best memories of my life are from that period.

> *O' the good memories of Tehran*
> *Those garden alleys of Shemran*
> *Where the sound of the rain, reverberated through the rain spouts*
> *The smell of Jasmine everywhere*
> *Porches full of flowerpots*
> *Homes with open door, loved to receive guests*

My older daughter had been admonished and interrogated on several occasions for letting some hair show under her scarf; despite all my daily warnings, she had in one of her school essays blamed the Shah for leaving Iran in the hands of a group of murderers. Thank God, her teacher called me in and said that she would ignore the matter that one time, and it passed. My younger daughter who pretended to be a boy was growing up and could no longer pass as a boy.

Controlling the children was becoming more difficult as time went by. Once the eight-year old son of a neighbor had mistakenly yelled out "death to Khomeini" instead of "death to the Shah," his poor mother went through hell, had to go to the Islamic committees' numerous times to praise the Imam. Do you think they would easily let go of a case like that?!

On the other hand, my eight-year old son, a student at the Nezam Mafi School, wrote such a passionate essay about the revolution that the school asked him to read the essay aloud in front of 2,000 students at the morning assembly. The next day, the school administration called to praise my son. They predicted that he would make a very good preacher with his influential command of the audience. I said to myself: "Over my dead body." All I need is a preacher son on a pulpit! (speaking ironically, she recites Hafez): *"Rejoice o' heart, the coming of Christ-like speaker!"*

The situation was getting worst by the day and the repression more intense. We saw fit to leave Iran for a better future.

> *My homeland is no longer thriving*
> *Freedom left, there is chaos everywhere*
> *Pain and sorrow replaced happiness*
> *Iran is not the same as before.*

In the Summer of 1989, we left Iran by land. We were told that the land route was safer. I have many nice memories of my last moments in Iran. The memory of a guard who told my young daughter to hide her favorite cassette music tape in her purse, to avoid having them confiscated. Or the memory of another guard who handed me my pieces of jewelry and said: "Put these in your pocket so that they are not visible. May God protect you and your children." Those were bitter moments: Hearing "may God protect you" from a fellow countryman made me burst out in tears. In the old days they would put a curse on someone by saying: "may you be adrift from your homeland." I guess someone had put a curse on us.

> *I have many good days, I remember everything*
> *I have a fistful of cherished earth from Iran as a souvenir*
> *Wherever I travelled to, my heart longed to return*
> *You don't know how hard it was to spend those days and nights*

We kept going and going and going; finally, on an evening with a full moon, we reached Vienna. I will never forget how on the very first night, I woke up screaming with the sound of an explosion. I thought we had been bombed but soon noticed that the sound was that of a garbage truck. My mind was still in Iran and war.

In Vienna, we rented a place. My husband took a job and my older daughter started school. We did not like living there. The memories of war were everywhere. In fact, we didn't like Vienna and Vienna didn't like us. Too often we were reproached for being foreigners.

> *Our Journey from the beginning*
> *was full of ups and downs*
> *Many times I asked God*
> *to make tomorrow a better day.*

We didn't stay in Vienna for long. soon, our papers were ready to emigrate to the United States. The United States took us with open arms. We started a new life, rented an apartment, put our children in school. Life was on a roll.

Soon it was time for me to find a job. I started working as a volunteer at my son's school. One day the school principal asked me to speak with an Iranian boy who was violently bullying the other kids and disrespecting his teachers. I found out that the poor child had domestic troubles. He told me, "In Iran we had a big house. My brother and I each had a room, here all of us sleep in the same room. My parents fight all the time, we don't have any friends or relatives. We don't have ANYBODY here, ANYBODY."

This incident made me start an association of Iranian mothers at the school to help the children and to guide the mothers to learn from each other in dealing with immigration issues. The school principal was really impressed with me. I also took courses in education and received a diploma that allowed me to get a job at another high school as an employment counselor for developmentally disabled youth. The students were twenty or twenty-one years old, but were developmentally comparable to eight-year-old children. My job was to find them employment so they can be part of society and increase their self-esteem. It was at this school that I noticed the high number of Iranian students.

On my first Nowruz [Iranian New Year on the first day of spring] I helped organize a Nowruz celebration with the help of other mothers. You would have loved one of the traditional Nowruz dishes that I prepared for it.

Back then, Nowruz was not as fashionable as it is now when the President and the Mayor deliver greetings and read from the poetry of Saadi; I had to struggle to explain each of the seven items traditionally placed on the table for this celebration. I asked each Iranian who had some means to pay for part of the cost and help with part of the labor. You would have loved the very respectable celebration that we organized. This very Nowruz celebration made the school and other students view Iranian students with more respect.

> *I smell the scent of spring and Nowruz.*
> *Let's take a fresh breath,*
> *Open the cage door and let the lovebirds out.*
> *If there is any bitterness in our hearts,*
> *Let's give it away to the wind*
> *Let's teach love and friendship all over again*

At the same time, I was finding jobs for my developmentally disabled students. For an Iranian girl who liked to wear heavy makeup, I found a job at an Iranian-owned beauty salon. The business owner claimed that the girl made more in tips than the owner earned in income. For a youth who liked to organize everything in clusters, I found a volunteer job at a copy shop which later permanently employed him. The copy shop owner also donated a copy machine to the school to boot. He said that: "It is our duty to help the school because our children are studying there. We have to show our appreciation." Iranians offered much cooperation and employed most of my kids in their operation.

The luckiest student was Kyle, the one with a heavy stutter who loved animals. I begged a pet shop owner to hire him. Soon he became the best salesperson. And his stuttering almost disappeared. One day a network television crew came to interview Kyle; they asked me to be there as well. That was followed by awards and appreciation letters. It made me so happy to know that I was helping the kids. Those were good times. I felt useful. I did all I could to pay my dues to this country.

> *Wherever I am, let me be, the sky is mine*
> *The window, the mind, the air, the love, the earth, are all mine*
> *What does it matter if, mushrooms of nostalgia grow from time to time?*
> —Sohrab Sepehri[3]

Now I no longer work outside the home. My husband is ill and needs my attention and care. My children are married and have given me grandchildren who also need my care. You know, parents were really harmed by this revolution. Perhaps other parents feel the way I do, a feeling of illiteracy. I feel deficient because I could never be a good-enough educational counselor for my children. I could never be the resourceful mother that I was in Iran; but the time has been spent well.

If there is any torment, we have seen it, If there is any anguish, we have felt it
Like an empty clay flower pot on a windowsill, we are filled with fractured memories
—Gh. Aminpour[4]

Now with the unrest in Iran [she is referring to the 2009 Green Movement], I worry a lot about the youth and about the mothers. On the night when they killed Neda, I cried a lot. One night I dreamt that I was watching Mount Damavand with its majesty and with snow on its peak. Suddenly I saw a husky man dressed in nomadic tribal attire, carrying a large dry tree trunk on his shoulders, coming down the mountain with determined strides. He planted the dry tree trunk by the side of a river; the tree grew, flourished, and became fruitful at an amazing pace.

I don't know how you would interpret my dream., but I have a premonition that Iran will once again become green and proud.

Wolves beware—in this strange tribe, though the tribe's leader is dead, his rifle remains
Though all the tribe's men were killed, there is a child in a cradle who still survives
—Zahra Rahnavard[5]

NOTES

1. Babak Radmanesh, "Chegooneh Zendegi Kardan" (How to live life), (n.d.), http://life-mahin.blogfa.com/tag/%D8%A8%D9%88%DB%8C%D8%B2%D9%86%D8%AF%DA%AF%DB%8C (accessed October 26, 2019).

2. Hadi Khorsandi, "Ghalam Charkhid" (The pens turned), (n.d.), http://www.asghara gha.hadikhorsandi.com (accessed October 26, 2019).

3. Sohrab Sepehri, "Sedaye paye ab" (The sound of water's footsteps), (n.d.), http://sher-farsi1.blogfa.com/category/2 (accessed October 26, 2019).

4. Gh Aminpour, "Goldan-e Khali" (Empty vase), (n.d.), http://shereno.com/poet-33 40.html (accessed October 26, 2019).

5. Zahra Rahnavard, "Gorgha" (The wolves) (n.d.), https://news.gooya.com/politics/ar chives/2009/06/089067.php (accessed October 26, 2019).

Eleven

Asal (Honey)

Homayoun Houshiarnejad

In Iran, I was in charge of the performing arts theaters in Tehran University. In the early stages of the revolution, I felt the catastrophic tragedy of the situation and saw fit to voluntarily resign from my position. I had served twenty years on the job and decided to retire ten years earlier than the government norm.

I did another revolutionary thing as well: I married my wife and rescued myself from a lifetime of loneliness. This was my second marriage, my first wife and our two daughters had immigrated to the United States after our divorce, a few years before the revolution.

> As the night pulled the blanket from the sun
> My heart filled with joy
> The garden of my heart bloomed
> And spoke loving words
> It fell in love with your eyes
> Cupid's arrow hit the target
> You are the belief, you are the partner
> You are the flame and the embers
> You are the first, you are the last
> You are the savior, you are the crown jewel
> —Homayoun Houshyarnejad[1]

In the beginning of the revolution, I had two hobbies. One was listening to foreign radio broadcasts, the other, painting. In the evenings, when I'd had enough of my activities, I would walk from my home in Vanaak Square all the way to Shah Street, where my father used to have a furniture store long ago. From there, I would catch the bus back home. In this way, I would savor my childhood memories for myself.

One day when I was at home, turning the radio dial, I came upon an Israeli station broadcasting a song by Shifteh, a Persian singer.

(epic lyrics about Persia)[2]

Listening to the song had a surreal effect on me: hastily I rose to my feet, got dressed, and, just like a soldier, I began to steadily march down the street, loudly singing this song.

On the way back, I continued singing, even on the bus, to the point where the driver stopped the bus and said: "Dear sir, for God's sake, get off the bus before you get all of us into trouble." Urged by the other bus passengers, I disembarked, but the effect of the music and lyrics of the song stayed with me. I thought to myself: what a beautiful thing I discovered, how a voice with suitable music and lyrics can have such a profound effect on a human being.

After many years, I once again began to write poetry. I say "again" because when I was young, I composed a collection of poetry called *Rahavard*. I was published, but to be frank, I saw that I could not support a wife and children with poems and poetry, so I went after clerical jobs.

One day, during my everyday stroll, I caught sight of a practically empty Café Naderi that was once a gathering place for writers, poets, and other open-minded individuals back in the day. Everything about it was dead. My heart sank. I thought to myself: If my father were alive today to see this, what would he have said? Wouldn't he have asked me: "Homayoun, what have you done to the shining homeland that I handed down to you?"

This thought stayed with me and would not let go. That night, we were at a party; I felt restless the entire night. I was so restless; I was like a pregnant woman about to go into labor at any moment and could not sit still. After a short while, I told Pouri, my wife: "get up and let's go home; I'm about to explode. I need to sit somewhere and write." We came home and Pouri went to sleep, but I stayed up until morning until the poem "Ghesaye Khak" (The Tale of the Soil) was born; a tale from the history of Iran. This poem became like social lubricant or, what musicians call, our potboiler. I was invited to party after party to recite my poem.

> *If today your whole being has been dissolved*
> *If today your palace of pride has been stripped of its foundation*
> *Then you must stand as strong as a mountain*
> *Grow as tall as a Cedar*
> *Become a pathway to the sun*
> *And build a new point to pray, named hope*

In one of these parties, a colonel came and as he was complimenting my poem, he told me: "Be careful that your poetry doesn't cause you any trouble. It's better that you leave Iran as soon as possible." I told him that in fact, I had already submitted my passport for permission to travel overseas and was waiting for a response. That very night, the colonel took my information and, three days later, my passport and Pouri's passport arrived at our home.

I should also add that, I used to travel regularly to America to visit the two daughters I had with my first wife. In 1978, I obtained a frequent entry visa that was set to expire in ten days. We left our home and belongings and set out for our first stop: Germany.

Oh the moments when we were about to board the airplane! I was constantly afraid that my name would be flagged somewhere, because honestly, one night I had thoroughly cursed out our mosque's prayer announcer. My heart was about to explode. All at once I saw the same colonel with plain-clothes officers who, without formal inspection, passed in front of us.

Pouri went as well, but a bunch of inspectors stopped me from going. They first searched my suitcase inside out, and then they gave me a hard time about why I had two rings on my hand. I jokingly replied: Sir, I have two wives; one of them is with me right now and I'm taking her to meet the other one! They finally let me go, but I was in such a state when I reached my seat on the plane. It's a story that still puts a lump in my throat.

> *Whatever has broken has broken, let it go*
> *Don't let yourself be broken today*
> *Whatever has passed has passed, let it go*
> *Whatever happened yesterday has passed*

We stayed with my sister in Germany. The next day, I went by myself to the American consulate; I showed them my passport and asked, "I still have a few days left on my visa; can you extend my visa so I can go to the United States? I would like to travel around Europe with my wife." They said, "No; you better go to America, since it's uncertain whether you can get another visa."

Our big mistake was that Pouri went to the consulate by herself two hours after I did where they asked her, "Where's your husband?" She replied, "In Iran." The counselor said "Really, then whose husband was here two hours ago?" He then put a rejected stamp on her passport. Consequently, Pouri stayed in Germany while, a few days later, I traveled to Los Angeles to stay at my brother's house.

Since I had journalistic experience, in the first few days I went to see my old friend, Manook Khodabakhshian, who was in those days, the editor of *Rayegan* (*Free*) magazine. He was happy to see me and said: "I'm short-handed, let's work together but know that there's no pay!"

The magazine office was located very far from where I lived. I asked Manook not to give this unpaid job to anyone else until I got a car. Since the money was good, and I was afraid of loosing it!

I went to San Francisco to see what was going on there, and I bought an ancient Chevrolet for $700 and drove it back to Los Angeles After the car overheated three or four times, I finally got to LA and that old rust-bucket became my crutch.

Each day, I drove over an hour-and-a-half to and from my brother's house to the *Rayegan* magazine office to work for free. Meanwhile, I was paying constant attention to poetry and songwriting. I realized that long form poetry did not work for me and started writing short poems.

Since *Rayegan* was the only Iranian publication at the time, it became the gathering place for singers, musicians, artists, and creatives. One day, the famous Iranian composer Ataollah Khorram came to the newspaper office. Manook introduced me to him and said: "This friend of mine came recently from Iran, he writes poetry beautifully, and he's chewed my ear off from reciting it day and night. Can you see if his work can be of any use to you?" Mr. Khorram gave me a look and said, "Well, well, how are you? What do you have?" And I said, "What do *you* have?" He said, " I have a song that has been recorded by Ms. Homeyra [famous Iranian female singer], but she is not fond of the lyrics. I'm looking for new lyrics to replace them with. Then I sincerely put forward whatever I had. When he got to the second lyrics, he said, "Hey, it seems like this one will work."

He gave me the address of his studio and told me to stop by after work. I went to the studio. Mr. Khorram kept playing the score over and over, I couldn't figure out what was what! But in order to hide and not show that I didn't understand, I kept nodding my head and saying "mm-hmm, beautiful, beautiful." At the end of the session, in order to find out what was happening, I said, "Now you sing this once yourself—see if the lyrics match the music. I think it most certainly will!" Mr. Khorram sang it, and I saw that the lyrics went hand in hand with the music. He sang, and it made my heart melt. Khorram said, "Let's pray that Ms. Homeyra likes it." That night I was worried and couldn't sleep.

The next day, around four or five in the afternoon, I heard the good news that Ms. Homeyra did indeed like the lyrics and the deal was made. I cannot describe how I felt at the recording session that night. I was dizzy with glee; I was in the clouds. So much so, that on my way back home, I absentmindedly drove 100 miles north, instead of south! This was my first job.

> *Being with you, my dear homeland, is my hope.*
> *Being without you, is the death of a garden,*
> *A flower estranged from its branch*
> *Being with you, my homeland, is the pleasure of poetry and stars*
> *Remembrances of beautiful nights, is a never-ending story*

A few days later, Shamaizadeh [another famous Iranian composer] came to the newspaper office. Again, Manook started singing my praises; enough that Shamaizadeh invited me to coffee so I could share my poems. Even before we sat, he said, "Mr. Houshiarnejad, if what you have is rubbish, I'll immediately tell you very straightforwardly! Don't get offended." I recited a few poems, and he didn't say anything, until I got to "Sarbaaze Koochooloo" ("Little Soldier") that was about child soldiers that went to warfronts. Suddenly he was bursting with joy, and he took me to his house. As soon as he opened the door, he told his wife, "I've brought someone who exudes poetry with his very being, and what poetry it is!"

He sat by the piano, tickled the ivories a little, and called Aref [another Iranian famous singer]. To make a long story short, the cassette, "Sarbaaze Koochooloo," came out, and it became my big break.

> *Little soldier, today's tale full of sorrow*
> *Little soldier, yesterday's small bird*
> *Little soldier, tomorrow's dawn light*
> *A withered branch of hope in the heart of the desert*

After a while, Manook left *Rayegan* magazine and took the name with him. For five years, I became the editor of a publication named *Fogholadeh* (Special Edition). Later on, I started to publish *Asre Emrooz* (*This Evening*) *which is now* more than thirty years old.

Let me tell you about my wife, Pouri, who has quite a story herself! Ms. Pouri called from Germany one day and said, "I've found someone who will take $3,000 in cash to get me an American visa." With complete confidence, she added, "Homayoun, he won't do this for just anybody! Because he's your sister's friend, he'll do us this favor!" I didn't waste any time; that very day I wired the $3,000. Two days later, in a craze, I went to the airport to pick up Ms. Pouri.

> *Extra! Extra! Read all about it!*
> *She is coming from afar*
> *The one who, on the roads of love*
> *No one had heard from*
> *She is coming from afar*
> *I pray she's not late*
> *nor stuck on the road*
> *I pray she comes soon*
> *From wherever she is and was*
> *From the road of love and affection*
> *With all her soul she comes*

At the airport, while I was impatiently counting the minutes before I could see Pouri, I suddenly heard my name being called on the loudspeaker! My heart sank! I went and saw that, yes, Ms. Pouri was arrested because of having a fake visa stamp on her passport! The two of us were in such a state, I cannot describe. They kept Pouri that night.

The next day, we went with a lawyer and bailed Pouri out. The lawyer could get her political asylum, but Pouri was so hurt by this "welcome" that she had no desire to stay in America. She insisted that she wanted to go back to Iran. My pleading was not effective. Almost two weeks later, Pouri called from Tehran and said: I'm pregnant! One came, two left. I thought to myself: Look, for God's sake, people risk their lives to come to America to have their children. Our Pouri goes from America to Iran to have our baby?!

> *In the name of the one that you worship*
> *I love you wherever you are*
> *taking account of my life*
> *Wherever I looked, there you were*

Pouri's pregnancy was during the Iraq war bombings, under the canopy of rockets, missiles, and destroyed buildings. Until finally on September 29, 1984, our daughter was born. Pouri chose the name "Asal" (Honey) because her eyes were the color of honey. Aref threw a giant party in honor of my new fatherhood and invited all the Iranian artists in town. In the middle of the night, when everyone was gone, I slept in the room for vagabonds, also known as a guest bedroom. I can't say I really slept, though; I tossed and turned all night long. I was happy to be a father, but I missed my family. My heart yearned for seeing Pouri and Asal. That very night, I wrote this poem for my daughter:

> *My sweet honey-eyed little girl*
> *Let me not see you left all alone*
> *I'm here in this corner of the world, and you in the other*
> *I don't know, when you opened your eyes, why I fell apart*
> *Who sang you lullabies and was called father?*
> *I wasn't there when they cut the cord*
> *I don't know how far they drew a life for you?*
> *My dear daughter, if there were no place left for anyone in this land*
> *You always have a place on your father's eyes.*

This very poem became the basis for another lyric, "Asal," sung by Davood Behboodi [famous Iranian singer] and was one of my most famous works.

My lyrics gained many fans. There were hardly any albums coming out without at least three to four of my lyrics in it. I was writing nonstop. It was as if they were being revealed to me, or that they were writing themselves, and I was just gathering them. My only concern was being away from Pouri and Asal. I discussed this with my old friend, Heshmat Mohajerani, who used to be the coach of Iran's national soccer team before the revolution. Mohajerani lived in Dubai and had a successful life for himself. He invited Pouri to Dubai and threw a large party for her and invited the American consular. He told the consular our story and asked for help. The next day, Pouri got the U.S. visa stamp in her passport; this time it wasn't fraudulent. Asal was six months old when Pouri came to America, and we chose Los Angeles as our home.

Many years have passed; Asal is now a doctor and *Asre Emrooz* magazine is over thirty years old. It hasn't been a bad life.

NOTES

1. The poems in this story are by Homayoun Houshiarnejad, *Baghe Alefba* (Garden alphabets) (Los Angeles: Asre Emrooz Publishing, 2007).
2. See Sarah Auliffe, "Popular Music and the Construction in Iranian Diasporic Contexts," *Context* 35/36 (2010–2011): 59–76, https://cpb-ap-se2.wpmucdn.com/blogs.unimelb.edu.au/dist/6/184/files/2016/07/35-36_Auliffe-27hcai8.pdf (accessed October 26, 2019).

Twelve

Living a Full Life

Iran

I was born in 1919 into an aristocratic family. My father was a state governor and renowned for his integrity and honesty. He was an excellent speaker and highly educated. He was fluent in French. At home he kept *Les Miserables*, by Victor Hugo next to his copy of the Koran. He would spend hours analyzing the characters in the book for us in French!

My mother was a gracious lady, obsessed with cleanliness. An excellent manager, and very avant-garde! My father always encouraged her. His death affected her deeply; she lost her greatest supporter. Now that her husband was gone and would soon be forgotten, she didn't want to be set aside. So, she got involved with social work and joined the Red Lion & Sun Society [Iran's equivalent of the Red Cross] as a volunteer.

> *Childhood memories were sweet,*
> *pure with no grudges*
> *Time passed, and only the memories remain*
> *Wish someone could bring back those good old days*

I was four or five years old when I was enrolled at the "Franco-Persian" School. I started to write using my left hand; the French teacher stuck a pin in my hand to punish me. I came home and told my mother. She stormed to the school and complained, saying: "I will let my daughter stay here only because there are two months left of the academic year. After that I am taking her to another school! I won't leave my child in a school that discriminates between the right and left hands."

I learned to drive at sixteen but didn't get my license 'til 1947 when I was twenty-seven. Dressing well was important to me; I was quite athletic, I was

117

a good tennis player, I rode horses, skied, and swam. I always had to walk around with a book, a habit inherited from my father.

I graduated high school in 1935 and started at the Painting Academy. After a few months, Reza Shah ordered women to remove the chador, opening the way for them to attend university. Long coats and hats had been imported from Europe by the government, and officials at the ministries held receptions inviting both men and women. Women would attend these events with their long coats and hats.

My father once hosted one of these receptions. He was modern and Muslim at the same time. He told my mother, "You know, the whole world doesn't wear a chador, you don't have to either." She removed her chador and that was that!

> *Oh you wicked little fox, I am a lioness*
> *Stay silent, I am enlightened*
> *Don't you dare use religion as weapon*
> *To burn down all that I am*

As soon as the universities started to admit women, my mother said: "Your high school diploma is worthless. It is time you had a university education, just like your brothers." My sister and I were among the first group of women to attend Tehran University.

Many couples met and married while at the university. But I wasn't thinking about marriage and not interested in boys until I met Bahman for the first time at our house in Shemiran. He and a cousin arrived unannounced one day. They said their family was looking to buy a property in Shemiran, so they had dropped in on us! Bahman was very good looking with big blue eyes. He was young and his capital was his youth and determination. He knew French and English, had a degree in business, and wonderful handwriting. To make a long story short, we got married in 1943 and God blessed us with two girls and a boy.

> *Sounds of children reverberated through the house*
> *Sounds that signify love*
> *Sounds of crying and laughter*
> *Sounds of happy pure children*

Bahman loved the kids. When he came home from work he loved to play with the children. He would change our son's diaper even though the nanny was standing there. We had several staff at home: a nanny, a cook, and a gardener. Among them, Kazem was exceptional. He was a tall, well-built young man from the villages and super-smart. When I saw how intelligent he was, I taught him to read and write and he was able to finish middle-school.

I helped all our staff learn to read and write. I don't want to brag, and I don't need the credit. It was my duty. When you are educated and the other person is not, it is as if you have food and another has none. It is your duty to feed the hungry. Later, Kazem married a wonderful young woman, bought a piece of land with his savings, and built a home. Before I left Iran, I found him a government job so he would have financial security.

Whatever I could, I did it wholeheartedly
As little as I could, I did my best

We raised our children in the modern style; the girls had dance and piano lessons and our son was sent to a Swiss boarding school when he was fourteen. We always used to celebrate their birthdays in a big way . . . we would decorate the whole house and send out invitations to their friends. Occasionally, it would be a costume party and sometimes we would hire an entertainer. We had quite a busy social life but entertaining and going out never interfered with taking care of the kids. I always oversaw my children's education and supervised their homework.

As for me, I was involved with charity work and I taught French twelve hours a week for fifteen years, at the high school. French was becoming less popular and English was replacing it as the second language. I had learned English in Tehran but was not confident about my command of it. When I realized the days of the French language were coming to an end, I signed up for a Fulbright scholarship and was among the first ten candidates to be accepted. I took advantage of the Fulbright scholarship and enrolled at the University of Michigan for a six-month course.

When I returned from the United States, Melli University had just been built on the hills of Shemiran. I was invited to teach English at the Science Faculty. I taught eight hours a week for the next eleven years. Of course, in addition to that, I was President of the International Women's Club (IWC) of Iran, my dear. During my tenure at IWC, we built a children's convalescence home. Her Majesty had donated 5,000 square meters of land to the Club on the condition that we build on it within three years.

My daughter drew up the architectural plans, pro bono. I encouraged my friends to each name a bed after themselves by donating 10,000 tomans to the convalescence home. Since people knew that every penny donated would be spent on the project, we managed to collect 700,000 tomans ($100,000 in those days). The Leila Convalescence Home was built.

I also was President of Zonta Club of Iran for a few years; all the members were women and it was affiliated with the International Zonta. We published a book listing the administrative and social services run by women in Iran.

Thus, you'd know my life and soul,
Extend a hand and aim to understand my role
O! You, the bitter piece! Except me as one with yours
I am of a different kind, but equal one with yours
Open your wings, and feathers, such is in the way of love,

And as such, I am the remex, if you are the wing of flight

Bahman and I lived together for thirty years, 'til he got seriously ill and died. I wore black for a year and since then I haven't been touched by a man!

My heart has not fallen for anyone, no one's heart has fallen for me
Like driftwood carried by the waves, I am free, free, free
I have no eyes for anyone, and no desire to raise my cup to the memory of lover
—Simin Behbahani[1]

I became aware of a lump under my breast mid-1978. My doctor suggested I should go to the United States for treatment at the Mayo Clinic. I quickly packed for a month's trip. My suitcase contained two day-dresses, two evening dresses, two long pants, two skirts, two jackets, two pairs of boots, two pairs of shoes, two handbags, one black one white—It made me think of Noah's Ark with its animals, a pair of each, a male and a female.

On the morning of 24th November 1978, Hajieh Khanom, the cook, passed to me the Koran and then poured a bowl of water, in which a green leaf floated, behind me on the steps of the house. I left the beautiful home, which was the fruit of thirty-five years of life, not knowing it would be the last time I would see it.

It was my fate to go on a journey, goodbye, goodbye, and I took my chances, goodbye, goodbye
I won't stay here any longer, goodbye, goodbye, oh, my dear ones, goodbye, goodbye
—Younes Salimi[2]

I was in the United States when I read and heard the news of the unrest in Iran. I wanted to return immediately, but both my daughters decided that I should go to Paris and stay there awhile.

We did not come for fame and fortune
We came for shelter from ill
—Hafez[3]

I was confused and lost; the newspapers announced that the Shah was heading for the United States for treatment. I was in Europe, but all my thoughts were with Iran—wondering what was happening to my homeland. I was having nightmares.

My sister and two of my uncles, each ended up spending four months in prison. My sister was banned from leaving the country for six years, and eventually was forced to pay a huge ransom to leave Iran. She wrote in her prison diary: "Each time I heard the shots from a firing squad, a young prison guard would gleefully announce 'Mother, it is your turn next!'"

We cried from dawn to dusk, we cried every step of the road
As they chopped down each poplar tree in the garden, we cried with each strike of the axe
—Qahaar Assi[4]

In Paris, we faked living! We gathered together with Iranian friends and discussed the political situation endlessly. Then the women decided to roll up their sleeves. . . . Conversations which used to be about fashion changed to discussions about recipes, food shopping, and residence permits. The men, however, continued to talk, interpret, and predict the political situation sitting in the cafés, and didn't go far. Though I knew Paris well, life was truly depressing in those years. The phone would be silent for days on end; I was bewildered and restless.

I tried to keep myself busy, twice a week I would play bridge . . . once with Iranian friends and the second time with my French friends. I read, went to the movies, ballet, and theater. . . . I did some sightseeing. Despite all this activity, I suffered from insomnia and felt my life was wasting away.

> *All I suffered from was homesickness*
> *The only balm needed was an intimate*
> *The only cure is my homeland*
> *Iran was the only homeland*

In 1980, to put an end to the feeling of uselessness, I attended Professor Rene Pomeau's lectures at the Sorbonne. Twice a week I attended evening classes at the Louvre. This way, I managed to fill up five days a week.

I decided to pursue a PhD in French Literature. Of the ten topics I listed for my thesis, my professor chose Andre Maurois, as "not much has been written about him." I did intensive research in libraries and museums for my thesis. Finally, on December 16th, 1985, it was time to defend my thesis. In it, I had referred to Balzac, stating that he was a good writer even though he was a heavy drinker. One of the members of the jury asked me, "How well do you know Balzac?" I said, "I know him well enough to have translated *Eugenie Grandet* into Farsi at the age of twenty-one!" The next member of the jury complimented me on the thesis as well as on my command of French. He said, "We have rarely seen anyone outside of these four walls who speaks French as well as you do." In the end, Professor Pumeau announced that my thesis had been accepted with honors. If I tell you that my depression was cured as a result of my studies, it would not be an exaggeration.

> *I was happy so long as I was around books,*
> *Teaching and school*
> *Feeling fortunate so long as education was my tool*

I have kept thirty-five journals over the years, each over 200 pages, I want to read you from some of them. Just so you know, I have always treasured human dignity and moral values over and above everything else, especially in the years after the revolution.

Paris, March 21st 1985: the first day of Farvardin. The radio kept announcing the beginning of spring. This was the first Nowruz I was spending in Paris. All morning I had been receiving phone calls from friends. I finally had an opportunity to contact the TV station, TF1 just before the 1 p.m. news and asked to send a message to the news reader—Yves Mourousi. I introduced myself and said I was an Iranian and a Muslim. . . . I then said "you have been mentioning the start of spring all day but you don't seem to know that today is the Iranian New Year—Nowruz." Then I spelled Nowruz for him and said, "Please tell the newscaster that it may be a good idea to congratulate the more than 40,000 Iranians living in France on the occasion of their New Year." I hung up. Just then a friend called to wish me a happy new year. I shared the story with her. She replied, "What an optimist you are; sadly, these days Iran has lost its importance here." I turned on the TV. The news was beginning. After the international and national news, I heard the announcer say, "Today is the first day of spring, the weather is perfect. I want to take this opportunity to wish a Happy Nowruz to all the Iranian residents in France. This day has long been the beginning of the new year for the Iranians." That same evening, the news anchor, Christine Okrent, shared the news from Channel 2 accompanied by footage of Tehran and the bazaar.

Paris, August 25, 2007: Today, I was invited to a conference given by Raymond Barre, who had been Giscard d'Estaing's Prime Minister during the years of the Iranian Revolution. I went, planning to ask him some questions. I wore a very smart black dress with a bright red jacket—to be sure I would be seen clearly. One of the TV anchors chaired the meeting and many important French industrialists were in attendance. The subject of the meeting was whether France should take part in the war against Saddam. I noticed that the anchor kept referring to the Gulf and avoided using the word Persian. At an appropriate moment, I raised my hand. I took the microphone and addressed my first question to the anchor. "Why do you avoid using the name Persian Gulf and just keep saying Gulf? Don't you know that this Gulf has a name and that name has been and will continue to be the Persian Gulf for a very long time? Please don't drop the name Persian in favor of countries whose birth I have witnessed!" A few people clapped. I continued. "My second question is addressed to the Prime Minister. Don't you think, sir, that your support of Saddam Hossein at the time he was attacking Iran has resulted in the dilemma you face at present?" The Prime Minister replied, "Madame, I never said Arabian Gulf. . . . I looked at the map and read what it says there. However, others also have a claim." The anchor interrupted him and said, "Why don't you answer the second question. . . . Do you regret having abandoned the Shah?" The Prime Minister said, "The Middle East is a land of complex contradictions which we, in the West, cannot quite understand." He was avoiding my question. I interrupted him and said, "But politics is even more complicated than the Middle East. I was in Paris at the time of the revolution and saw how your help contributed to the success of the Iranian Revolution." He replied, "Mr. Khomeini was a political asylum seeker." I said, "There are plenty of asylum seekers here now. Does your government provide each of them with thirty-four phone lines and three live TV channels so they can express their views freely?" A few people clapped again. I sat down.

My land was once a fable
Unfamiliar with demons and devils
That precious land
Was a peerless gem

On November 4, 1992, fourteen years after leaving, I took an Air France flight bound for Tehran to see if I could salvage something from my life, my home, and sort out all the loose ends I had left behind. I found myself in two contrasting worlds under the same sky! During the day, I would be at the Revolutionary Council, facing miserable and scruffy human beings. . . . At night, as a guest at dinner parties in spectacular homes, I was met with fantastic hospitality and kindness. Surely, God created ugliness so we could appreciate beauty.

In order to recover a small part of what we owned, I made many unsuccessful visits to the Courts. The enormous dossier which represented a life's work of which I should have been proud, was now being used as an excuse to justify the injustice they wanted to force on me. I answered a hundred questions. The young prosecutor asked me if I wore hijab in Paris. I replied that I did not, since that would attract too much attention. He asked, "Mother, can you read and write?" I answered him in the same dialect, "A little!" He gave me a sheaf of papers to fill out. I sat on a metal chair in the hallway and started to answer the questions. After that, the oral examination began. Nevertheless, he sent me to another office for more fruitless questioning, then another and another. . . . Finally, after hundreds of Q & A's and four more trips to Tehran, I was able to recover my one-bedroom eighty-three square meter apartment! Now, at least, I had an address in Tehran. But the Iran I found was not the Iran I had known; that Iran was already dead.

The Mongol invaders should be absolved,
These vultures have made Iran hell
They took, devoured, and ripped apart everything
In the name of God, they smothered

My last trip to Iran was in 1997. After that I never returned and made up my mind that Paris would be my home, well until October 12, 2007. On that day, I said goodbye to the Paris apartment I had bought a few years before the revolution and which held all my memories of exile. And I said goodbye to French which was my second language and moved to San Francisco. I needed to be near my children. I lived by myself in San Francisco for five years. I cooked and received friends until I turned ninety. Suddenly, I couldn't do it anymore. I had no energy left. My son bought the house next door to one of my daughters. I have been living here for a few years. I'm ninety-seven years old, now I do nothing at all. Old age has its own problems. The only cure to old age is to die young.

> *If I ever come face to face with my youth*
> *I swear to my grey hair*
> *I will hold on to it, I will appreciate it.*

I don't keep a journal anymore because I really have nothing more to say. I lead a simple life. I have a small diary in which I keep track of what I need to do, so I don't forget—just for my own information. I am grateful to God; I have good children. I received a good education. I was always able to adjust to the life I had. I thank God for my intelligence and good heart and the fact that I have lived a life of truth; I am not bragging.

I have travelled far and wide and seen the whole world. I am grateful that my perspective on life has expanded considerably over the years. I am and have always been eternally grateful to the Almighty. He has provided for us so far and we have lived a dignified life.

In the past, speaking a foreign language was fun. Nowadays speaking English is a necessity. My daughter-in-law, one grandchild, and my great grandchildren don't speak and will never speak Farsi. Sometimes I just wish I could just speak pure Farsi for a whole day

> *Sometimes I yearn to speak in pure mother tongue*
> *I yearn for an extended "salam" instead of a "hello"*
> *I years for the scent of Jasmine and rose water from Kashan*
> *Sometimes I yearn to dream of childhood again*

Yes, it has been a good life. I am grateful to God the Almighty. I just don't know how to deal with the distances. . . .

NOTES

1. Simin Behbahani, "Delam gereftehh havaye geryeh" (I feel like crying), in *Dashte Arjan* (Tehran, Iran: Zavvar Publishing, 1991).

2. Younes Salimi, "Khodahafez, Khodahafez" (Goodbye, goodbye), (n.d.), http://shere-no.com/22000/20232/169062.html (accessed October 26, 2019).

3. Hafez, "Ghazal 365" (Sonnet 366), (n.d.), https://ganjoor.net/hafez/ghazal/sh366/ (accessed October 26, 2019).

4. Qahaar Assi, "Geristim" (We cried), (1989), http://qahaar-assi.blogfa.com/1386/06 (accessed on October 26, 2019).

Thirteen

A Space to Design

Manijeh Teymouri

I had no intention of immigrating, but destiny had other plans for me. My younger brother was getting married in Florida and sent the invitation; my mother and I easily got visas and entered America in June 1985.

We stayed in Florida for one month and then were invited to Sacramento by my aunt. My aunt and her family had been invited to a wedding, and when the hosts heard that we were staying with my aunt, they invited us to the wedding as well. It was one of those elaborate Iranian wedding parties.

They had almost 500 people guests. Hamid was one of them. Since there was never any good news coming from Iran, my mother and I thought it would be best if we stayed in America. We were on the fence about whether to go to Florida or to stay in Sacramento. We both decided to stay in Sacramento since the weather was nicer there was a love possibility!

> *I was captivated by him*
> *with all my heart and soul*
> *I was his confidant*
> *I fell head-over-heals for him*
> *I think I am in love with him*
> *I think I am in love with him*

Hamid was engineer. He had a government job. But he was capable of doing many things. He could take down a car engine and put it back together again. He was in love with cars. He called one day and said, "Manijeh, I'll come pick you up this evening; I have a surprise for you." My heart sank. I thought to myself, "Is he going to propose? I'm not ready for this. He should have talked to me about this. He should have said something. Previously, he had asked me once, "If I ask you to marry me, would you accept?" I had replied, "I like you very much, but for marriage, I will have to think about it." Now, all of a sudden, there's a surprise!?

I didn't push it with the questions, but I was in panic until he came. When Hamid came to pick me up that evening, I saw that he had bought himself a Porsche to surprise me! Every once in a while, Hamid found ways like this to surprise me. Another time, he surprised me by buying himself a boat!

With great gusto, he picked me up and took me for a ride. It was a tight squeeze with a lot of sharp turns; I was really scared and, honestly, did not feel good about it.

I wish we could capture our feelings in a photo
Put them all together in a frame of love
The feeling of falling in love . . . you and me becoming us . . . thinking of tomorrow

One rainy night, not too long after buying the Porsche, Hamid called and said, "I'll come pick you up tonight, let's go to dinner." I said, "I'm a little tired tonight. Can we go tomorrow night?" He replied, "Sure, I'll go drive around in my car and call you when I get home." I was awake until 11 [o'clock], and Hamid hadn't called yet. I thought to myself that maybe he had forgotten. But I was a bit worried because every night, before sleeping, we would chat on the phone for a short while. I fell asleep.

Early in the morning, I had a dream that one of Hamid's friends called me and told me that he had been in an accident and was in the hospital. At 7 a.m., I called his work. A man picked up, and I asked about Hamid. With shock in his voice, he said, "Hamid is in the morgue." At first I thought I had heard incorrectly. Maybe I was still dreaming. But no! I had heard correctly! This time, Hamid had really surprised me. I was broken. I couldn't believe it. For a long while, I was in shock. It was very difficult for me.

I wish we could preserve each moment of life
So, at the time of sorrow, we could look at happy mementos
The good days and . . . the times where we laughed and . . . the first kiss, and . . .

After Hamid's death, I couldn't stay in Sacramento. I came to Los Angeles to begin a new life. There are two things I haven't told you: one is that, while I was in Iran, I was a teacher, and, after the revolution, I decided to resign. The other thing is that when I was thirteen years old, I went to a sewing class and still sewed something every now and then. One time, I even sewed a wedding dress for one of the girls in my family. In Los Angeles, I met an Iranian lady who was a seamstress and was in need of some help to sew some clothes. I worked with her for a while, and, at her suggestion, I got my sewing license and started looking for work.

Looking for work in the newspaper, I found someone who was hiring a seamstress in downtown Los Angeles. I went to the ninth floor of a building for an interview. They had an order for eight evening gowns that had to be ready right away. They gave me pre-cut pieces for one dress, and a ready-made dress to duplicate, and have it ready in two days.

When I got on the elevator to come down, I saw a flyer posted in the elevator that someone on the fourth floor was hiring a seamstress. I went to the fourth floor for an interview. The lady in charge asked me, "How many years of work experience do you have?"

I thought she was asking, "For how many years have you known how to sew?"

I replied, "Twenty-five years." (It didn't end badly!)

She pointed at the clothes in my hand and asked, "Did you sew this yourself?"

I said, "No, this is a sample that I have to use to sew from."

She said, "Leave your phone number."

When I came home, I saw that she had left me a message telling me that I should come and work for her for a week as a test. I started work right away and was hired permanently after one week. She was pleased with my work. Especially because I didn't know how to say "no" to anything and I would take on more responsibility than what I was paid for. I worked there for years and got my Green Card with their help as well. But, unfortunately, I was forced to quit over a misunderstanding, I was heartbroken.

> *I was heartbroken and could take it no more*
> *I had seen enough of the good and the bad*
> *My heart had cut loose and needed to be left alone*
> *All alone*

For a while, I worked with a woman seamstress called Zaza. Zaza worked in Hollywood. She brought work home, and I would help her. One day, she told me, "Motion Picture has signed a contract with a company for the film, *Star Trek First Contact*, and they're looking for someone who has expertise in fabric and knows how to create sewing patterns."

It was always my dream to work in Hollywood, so I went for an interview. They told me that there was a group of twenty-five people who were working on this project who have found themselves in a bind: no matter how they change the sewing patterns, they can't figure out what's wrong. "Now can you tell us what's wrong with this sewing pattern?" As soon as I saw it, I said, "The problem is not the sewing pattern itself, rather, it's the fabric that's the problem. The fabric needs to have a bit of stretch to it." Immediately after, they signed a contract with me. They provided me with the fabric I requested. I prepared the costume. They took me to the film studio for fitting. When I saw the cast of *Star Trek*, it was as if I was taking a stroll through my childhood. It was as if I was in a dream. I couldn't believe it. The moment that Patrick Stewart put on his costume he said, "It's perfect." The entire studio burst into applause and started praising me, but I was dizzy in my own fantasy and couldn't hear anything.

> *I was in my childhood dream*

I was in my sweet simple dream
I was in the moon, in the starts, on the sky
I was the happiest person on earth

After that, my boss called me over and said, "Manijeh, since I was a child, I always dreamed of creating costumes for science fiction films. Now, I want to do the costumes for the film, *Apollo 13*. Are you ready to work with me as manager of this project?" Like I said before: I didn't know how to say "no," and I accepted the offer right away. I thought to myself that, no matter what, I would do whatever it took to learn this kind of work.

In order for me to see these kinds of clothes up close, they sent me to NASA. With great attention to detail, I viewed all the uniforms. In the span of three months, I sewed three sets of seven-layered clothing, exactly like the original. I worked incredibly hard and put a lot of effort into it. But, the night of the private screening, the tiredness had left and was replaced with pride; my feelings could not be expressed. Let me tell you, it's very exciting when you see your handiwork being worn by the stars of the silver screen.

As if my feet are not on the ground
there is nothing better than this
As if I am flying and I don't belong to earth

After this project, I sewed many costumes in other science fiction films, the most famous being *Contact*, with Jodie Foster starring, as well as *Space Cowboys* which was directed by Clint Eastwood who also had a starring role.

The first time Clint Eastwood saw me, he said, "Are you from Saudi Arabia?"

I replied, "No, are you asking that because of my accent?"

He said, "No, it's because, one time, for shooting a film, I went to Saudi Arabia and all the women were wearing niqabs and all you could see of them were their beautiful eyes. I always wondered, to myself, what kind of woman was behind this niqab. Today, your beautiful eyes reminded me of them." All of a sudden, I felt:

Blood rushed to my cheeks, I blushed
shame crept into my eyes, I panicked
Like a little kid slowly and gently
I got lost in my own world

I loved my work; however, from that same place inside me where I didn't know how to say "no," I took on more work than I was getting paid for. My work piled up so much that, after seven years, I left because I couldn't take the pressure any longer.

I was heartbroken and could take it no more
I had seen enough of the good and the bad
My heart had cut loose and needed to be left alone
All alone

Since I had worked for many years in this industry, I knew many people in Hollywood, who would bring me work occasionally. One of these people was Jennifer who worked with famous actors. One day, close to the Oscars, around 5 o'clock in the afternoon, she called me and told me to go to Angelina Jolie's house to help with her Oscar gown. (Many of the clothes worn at the Oscars are not sewn for a specific actor and need to be altered.)

At the beginning, I was really star-struck by the meeting of all these actors, and I worked hard so that I would not waste any opportunity. But, little by little, I saw that my days and nights were not mine anymore. Any time of day or night, Jennifer would get in touch with me and would send me here and there.

Not once did I say no! Always yes, sure, of course!
Years passed, but alas there was no cure for this pain

At the suggestion of my brother, one day I sat down and wrote "NO" a hundred times so that I would learn to say it out loud at least one of those times!

A hundred times I wrote no, 'til I was able to speak it once
It had to take all of me, before I learned my lesson

Eventually, one day, I called Jennifer. So that she wouldn't get upset, I talked myself down. I said, "I've gotten old. I don't have the energy. I can't work night and day to have the clothes ready in time. It would be good to look for someone else." She wasn't too pleased, but we are still in touch, and she gives the most difficult jobs to me.

It's been years now that I have my own studio. Now, instead of traveling to a client, clients come to me. My time is my own. I have my own unique clients. I've also hired a manager to take care of my financial needs who gives me the time to work tirelessly.

Overall, I'm happy about my immigration. Life has shown me that whenever someone does something to wrong me or something bad happens to me, it's because something good is just around the corner. For this reason, nothing ever bothers me; even the bad things. I just have to learn to, every once in a while, say "No!"

Fourteen

A Small Suitcase for a Great Escape

Modjgan Rashtian

My mom really liked for all us girls to work; that is why I majored in business. After I got my diploma, one day my mom asked our neighbor, Jaleh, "Do you know anywhere Modjgan could work?" Jaleh said: "Sure . . . Apadana Travel Agency is looking for a secretary."

They hired me on the spot; thanks to my great typing. That was where I met Behzad. We got very close. And he proposed! I'm sure you're all thinking to yourselves everything is all good now . . . no?!!! But that wasn't the case . . . there was just one tiny little problem. He was Muslim . . . and I'm Jewish!!!!!

What can I say. . .? I still don't get how I started on this journey. I guess you can call it falling in love . . . ignorance . . . foolishness . . . I have no idea, all I know is I got involved with Behzad and I lost all my senses

> *At first it was just his gaze*
> *A nice ring in his voice*
> *Then, bit by bit at one gesture*
> *I would give my life for him*

Honestly, I was not happy with my family. My mom always wished that I were a boy. Would you believe that I don't have a single picture of me as a kid???!! I have absolutely no idea what I looked like! But of course, my sisters have some of theirs; studio portraits where they pose with their hand under their chin and tilt their head! And then there's my brother . . . he has pictures from his own circumcision to his son's!!

But not me . . . the only picture I have was from my sister's wedding. I'm twelve or thirteen years old . . . standing next to my other sisters. It's completely clear that the photographer just wanted a shot of the bride with her sisters. And we were all striking a pose.

I don't know who I was or what I looked like
In the days when I loved lullabies
The days, when . . . there was innocence in my eyes
I loved those carefree days

One day Behzad and I were holding hands walking down Persepolis Street, when my dad passed us in his car and saw us!!!! I came home, and all hell broke loose, it was bad; my dad wanted to throw acid on my face. He said, "You are forbidden from going to work."

The thought of suicide crossed my mind, my parents decided to send me abroad . . . those were horrible days. I was confined to the home and did not have permission to go out. After a few days, my coworker Farzaneh called to check on me. I told her, "Tell Behzad to pick me up from my home tomorrow at seven in the morning so that we can run away together." Sometimes I say to myself, "What would've become of me if Farzaneh hadn't given my message to Behzad!!"

If the world was mine
If only one day was in my favor
If out of hundreds of destinies
I had a chance to write ONE
My fate would be better than this . . .

The next morning, I packed a little sack and escaped under the pretext that I was taking out the trash. We left Tehran for Kermanshah and stayed at his sister's home for two weeks. That was where I wore a white wedding dress, we had a minister come, and we got married. I have no clue how all this happened, all I remember is that I was very happy to be out of my parent's home.

My parents disowned me, they said, "Get lost and do whatever the hell you want!!!" And after the revolution, they went to the United States and I didn't hear from them. I was left with my naiveté and love.

I got pregnant very quickly and my daughter Saharnaz was born. Behzad was a nice man but I slowly realized he was distant and on drugs. I was nineteen years old and had never seen or smelled hashish or opium. I kept noticing Behzad's strange smell and sometimes he was spaced out.

Saharnaz was seven or eight months old when the conflicts between us surfaced. Around that time, Behzad and I were dispatched to London by the travel agency to open another branch. In London, Behzad really took things to the next level and started doing heroin and got arrested by the police. Opening a new branch of the travel agency was also cancelled due to the beginning of the revolution. In the midst of all this chaos, I got pregnant again!!! There was no one to tell me, "You idiot, stupid fool, what's up with you and your second kid??!" I'm telling you. . . . I was naïve and stupid.

The spring of my lifetime turned into autumn

It had been long since I had reached the end of my rope
But I kept silent until a day came when
Separation became the topic of our conversation

Behzad's family were aware of his problems and they honestly helped us a lot. They gave us one floor of their apartment to live in. His brother tried many times to get him to quit; had him hospitalized but he was beyond help. First, Behzad sold the rugs in our home, after that my jewelry went missing one piece after another. Our problems were only getting worse day by day when our second daughter Maryam was born.

Saharnaz had turned three years old and Maryam was fourteen months old; I was drowning in my life's problems when one day my aunt called and said, "What are you up to? Your mother is worried about you!" I told her the story. She said, "Your mom accepts you joyfully, but we must first figure out how to get you through to America." I thought about it and figured the only way out was to escape.

Once again, I packed up some clothes for myself and the kids in that same little sack, took my gold and valuables, and left for my cousin's home. I really did a good job by taking the deed to the home, I keep saying how naïve I was, but sometimes I knew what I was doing and acted wisely!

I gave my aunt the power of attorney to handle my divorce. Behzad's mother and brother really tried to convince me to go back; they wouldn't agree to the divorce. One day I called them and said, "If you don't agree to the divorce, I'll leave my kids here and take off!!" I wasn't serious, it just bluffing, and they folded. Behzad's brother called the next day saying, "Give us back the deed to the home and write in your divorce papers that the children will be in your custody until they turn eighteen, before we agree to the divorce." I accepted right away, and quickly got divorced.

All my intimate words, be they yours
All those lies and deceptions, be they mine
All the days of youth, be they yours
All the Memories, be they mine

At the start of the revolution, there were some groups that would smuggle Jewish people across the border. They took $2,500 from me to get me and my children across the border. Once again, I packed my little sack. Someone came and took us to Mehrabad airport. Before the flight, they took our passports and our money, and they said, "Once we've crossed the border, we will return everything to you." They also warned us not to talk to anyone on the airplane.

We went to Zahedan, a van picked us up from there. I noticed that thirteen of the airplane passengers were with us. A while later, the Revolutionary Guards blocked us from passing. The driver said, "My passengers have relatives in prison, and are going for a visit," and to persuade them, he put some money into their hands!!!!

We went a long way; eventually, we reached a dirt road where two Balochi men took us into a pickup truck. They sat me and my kids in the front and the rest sat in the back. I had only brought a few packs of cookies for the kids, and nothing else; but the people in the back, they came fully prepared with kookoo sabzi, pickles, bread, and garden herbs and shish kabob . . . they were fully prepared, as though they were there for a picnic.

It was dark everywhere, pitch black! As we were going, the driver suddenly hit the brakes hard. We all got out of the pickup and noticed that the truck was on the edge of a cliff, another inch, and we would have been at the bottom of the valley! And there was no Muslims among us to sing the praises of Allah, Mohammad, and his descendants (send a *Salavat)!* God had mercy on us!

The driver dropped us off by a cave; he gave us our passports and money as he entrusted us to another person. That person got us across the border and then sent us all to Karachi by plane. In Karachi, an Iranian Jewish lady picked us up and took us to a hotel. I was feeling a bit more relieved.

> *The road dust was still on my skin*
> *The noise in my head, still a din*
> *Alas, having barely arrived I could see*
> *What ominous days lay ahead therein*

I let my mom in America know I had crossed the border. My mom said, "Go to Israel first and stay with your cousin. He'll handle getting you to America." But she was pointing to the wrong direction, other Jews went straight to Austria to apply for asylum, from there they would apply for entry to the United States Though this is all just speculation.

To obey my mom's instructions, I went to Israel. My cousin said, "I know someone who will get you an American visa in exchange for $5,000!" I said, "Okay." A young man accompanied me and my kids to the American embassy in Tel Aviv. He showed the deed to his house and said to the consul in Hebrew "This is my wife and she wants to go with our kids to see her mother in America!" The consul was no idiot! Of course, he didn't buy it and said, "I will give your wife a visa to go with one child . . . and have the other child stay with you so you don't miss them all too much!"

Again, I called the mastermind of the family: my mother. She said, "Go to Mexico!" I immediately packed my so-called little sack and set out for Mexico; with much hurdles, I managed to get myself to a hotel over there and who do I call? My mom! My mom says, "Go to Tijuana!" I have no idea how I dared to do all these things. Believe me, there is no way I would ever dare to do all that again!

I went and bought a bus ticket, carrying my little girl in one hand and holding my big girl's hand with the other, and with that little sack over my shoulder, I was headed to Tijuana. We were going on a tight and narrow road for two days. Before our very eyes, a bus slid off the road and into the valley below and all the passengers went bye-bye.

The bus stopped somewhere along the way; apparently, we needed to have a tourist permit to pass through to Tijuana. The officer came and stood right above my head and said somethings, so I showed him my passport and he asked me where I was going. I said that my mother was coming to Tijuana and that I am going to see her! He told me to come with him. Saharnaz was asleep on the seat beside me; I left her on the bus and carried Maryam with me off the bus.

I had two $100 bills in my pocket because I had heard you have to give them money. They took me to a dark room where an interrogator was sitting behind an old wooden desk. It was just like what they show in movies. He asked, "What business do you have in Tijuana?" I said, "My mom is coming to San Diego to see us." He asked if I wanted to go with her and I told him no. He said, "How much money do you have?" I pulled out the two $100 bills from my pocket and he said, "Leave it and go." My whole body was shaking as I boarded the bus, we started back on our way. The bus stopped again one hour later; this time I put a $100 bill in my passport and gave it to the officer who then proceeded he calmly open my passport, take out the money and return my passport without any question.

We reached Tijuana early one morning. I'm not talking about the Tijuana where everyone goes for fun these days. I'm talking about the 1982 Tijuana, where you would have been terrified walking around!!

Can you guess who I called from there????!!! My mom, of course!

She said, "Alright, you made it! Go like a lady and take a taxi to bring you to San Diego." I was clueless about how things worked, I had just arrived from the other side of the world. So, I went and smoothly hailed a taxi, the driver pulled over and asked where I was going. I told him, "San Diego." He said, "Pay $150 and get in." I paid the money and sat carefree in the taxi. The taxi kept going and going way out of the city. I started panicking and took out a knife I always had on me, and held it in my hand, ready. Of course, it was just a knife I use for peeling fruit for the kids and that wouldn't be suitable for killing someone, but it was good to ease my mind. Then we reached somewhere with grass and barbed-wire fences as high as the sky, the car stopped, and the driver said, "Get out." I said, "No . . . San Diego!" He pointed angrily past the barbed-wire fence and said, "San Diego" which of course meant, I should dare to jump over the fence. I left the car out of fear; I thought he would kill us. Again, holding one kid in my arms and the other with my hand, we made our way on foot. We walked a long way on foot until finally a driver took us back to Tijuana.

My heart is sick of anything to do with travel
Anything to do with cities and roads
My heart is sick of all the hardened, unremorseful hearts
And sick of the beautiful, the ugly, the good and the evil

Again, I called my mom!!! She said, "For now, just stay in a hotel until I find another way." Two days later she called and said: "Ms. Rachel is coming with your aunt and cousin to smuggle you across the border." I asked who Ms. Rachel is. She said, "Don't you worry about a thing! Ms. Rachel has smuggled lots of people across the border."

The next day, Ms. Rachel, wearing heavy makeup and a fur coat, rolled up to my hotel to pick me up in a stretched American Chevrolet car, with my aunt and cousin in tow. My cousin and aunt, per Ms. Rachel's instructions, took my little sack which held everything my kids and I owned in this world and took off.

Ms. Rachel put a fur coat on me, so it looks like we're all rich. She then gave me my sister's driver's license and told me, "Try not to talk too much, let me do all the talking." Ms. Rachel and I sat in the car all chic in fur coats next to the kids as we reached the border. A lady asked for our green cards, Ms. Rachel remained unphased as she handed my sister's Driver license. The lady said, "I said green card." Ms. Rachel said, "It's not on her, it's with her husband; and her husband is in Los Angeles." The lady said, "Head into the station and tell him to bring her green card!" We went into the station. Thank God Saharnaz started to cry; perfect timing. The border patrol saw the kid wouldn't stop crying and said: "Go back to Tijuana for now, until your husband brings your green card!" If not for that, they would have made me go back to Iran right from there. We went back to the hotel. Ms. Rachel left. And that little sack went with my dear aunt. The kids and I were in the hotel for one week wearing the same clothes we had on our backs, just waiting to find out my mother's next bright idea for getting us into the United States

I must remain in wait,
To just sit and to pray.
If only I could read
The writing of my fate,
To erase a few scribbled lines
So here I would not stay

My mom informed me that a person with such and such traits would come pick us up to bring us across the US-Mexico border. It was just my luck it rained like crazy; it wouldn't quit for three days. It was muddy everywhere. Someone came after us and put us in a taxi with some other people sitting inside. He dropped us off at the foot of a hill and said, "You have fifteen minutes to get yourselves to the top of the hill." It was not easy to walk to the top with two kids. We were in the mud up to our knees. But we made it to the top. They shoved all of us into a big bathroom with a small window; there were thirteen of us.

U.S. helicopters flew over us every fifteen minutes, shining their search-lights. Everyone did their best to duck out of sight. We were on our feet for hours. Every so often, they called a few names and a few people would run outside. At 1:00 a.m. they called our names. We ran outside and into a van. They had folded the seats and closed the shades. We went a long way until they finally opened the shades and we saw an American flag. We knew we had crossed the border. We changed cars and drivers three more times until my primary connection took me to my parent's home.

I was a single person when I ran away from my parents' home. Here I was back at home with two kids. The smuggler also came inside. My mom brought tea and in her own special way told the smuggler, "My son in law immigration!" The guy obviously looked confused. My mom tried again to better state what she meant and said, "Daughter husband work immigration!" She wasn't lying, my brother-in-law worked for Immigration Services. But I still don't get why my mother insisted on making sure this smuggler knew this!!! Maybe she thought he would give her a special discount for immigration personnel!!! I have No idea! The only thing I remember was that, deep down, I was happy to finally reach the United States

I lived with my parents for a while . . . the entire time, they were just scolding me and making me feel guilty. I quickly applied for asylum, got a job, and left my parents' home. It wasn't an easy start to my new life, I really struggled before I was able to get a handle on life. The worst thing was I didn't get to enjoy my kids; there weren't many opportunities for me to spend time with them and to hold them, to kiss them, and I hadn't learned any of that from my parents or anywhere else.

When I was a kid, I wanted to get married, to have children, and to be a housewife, stay at home and raise my kids. Well . . . I reached some of those wishes and I dreamed about the rest. Anyway . . . I'm done with crying . . . I'm good now. . . . I have peace. My daughters are successful, they both got married and have their own lives; I have grandkids. I have been living by myself for years. It was hard for me at first and I thought that I couldn't do it, but now I like my solitude. I keep myself busy with grandkids, I read books, watch TV, and travel with friends. Overall, I have peace of mind. But honest-ly, every now and then I ask myself: "What would've been my destiny if Farzaneh, my co-worker at the travel agency, hadn't given my message to Behzad?!!"

> *If the world was mine*
> *If only one day was in my favor*
> *If out of hundreds of destinies*
> *I had a chance to write ONE*
> *My fate would be better than this . . .*

Fifteen

The Teacher

Sorour Nayeri

I am honored to be speaking to you as an Iranian woman who has tasted freedom. I was born during the time when woman had freedom under the great Reza Shah. I owe a lot to Reza Shah because he is the one who gave me freedom.

During all my time as a student in school, I was the top student. In second grade, in elementary school, I was the number one student in Shiraz. When I was in third grade, in elementary school, our teacher, Ms. Shiva, fell ill. The Ministry of Education didn't have any teachers to send in her place. Ms. Shiva introduced me to the school board and said that this student could teach the class. I said, "I will only agree on the condition that on the chalk-board there be a well-behaved/badly-behaved list and that the schoolmaster should punish the bad students!"

They agreed and I taught and took the class forward for three months. A few months later, the Iranian Cultural Minister came to Shiraz. They introduced me to him as the most prominent student. In order to show his appreciation, the Minister awarded me with a fifth-grade textbook as my prize.

In those days, textbooks were rare. With this book, I not only taught myself, but my sister and my cousin also learned from it as well. And these are just the ones that I know who studied with this book; God knows how many more studied with this book later. Do you remember when we used to recite what a book is about?

> *I am a kind friend, wise and eloquent, I speak of many things, though I can't talk*
> *I give you a lot of advise, and know about many things, I am an artist friend,*
> *I'm beneficial but not harmful*
>
> —Abbas Yamini Sharif[1]

My father was a merchant and the chairman of the Shiraz Chamber of Commerce. He was an open-minded man, but people's opinions were important to him as well. People started feeding him ideas: *Your daughter is grown up now. It's not right for her to go to high school!*

I went on a hunger strike for one month until my father finally gave in, and I registered for Shahdokht High School in Shiraz. I was the top student for all six years of high school. I took the entrance examination and got accepted into a medical program, but I did not have the temperament for the sight of blood. I then took the entrance exam for literature and got accepted. All through my time in university, I was also the top student each year.

During my last year, the top student was supposed to get a gold medal and travel outside of Iran to America in order to continue their studies; However, the son of a famous journalist in Tehran was unjustly introduced as the top candidate. In plain sight, they crossed out where it had said "Number One Student" on my report card and handwrote wrote over it, "Number Two Student" and handed it back to me! It was because of this injustice; I became sick and didn't get out of bed for a month.

My father became very upset and said, "It doesn't make sense that you're lying around; I'll send you to America myself. Go to Tehran and ask around to see how you can go to America."

I came to Tehran, stayed with my uncle and went to the Iran-America Friendship Society on Naderi Street and, with their help, got an acceptance letter to study at the University of Kentucky. And when was this exactly? Over fifty years ago! No one was going to America back then. They didn't know where Kentucky was! I got a plane ticket from Pan American for two weeks later, and my uncle came with me to the bus station on my way to Shiraz.

There, a tall, sharply-dressed, good-looking man approached us. He greeted my uncle and said, "I'm Borhan Ibn Yusuf."

My uncle recognized him and said, "Ah . . . are you Emadi's nephew?"

He said, "Yes, it seems like I have the pleasure of traveling with you today."

My uncle said, "Not me, but my niece is going to Shiraz. It's great that I ran into you; I entrust you with this girl."

My uncle let the fox guard the hen-house! I told my uncle, "Uncle, do you know this guy that you are leaving me with?"

He replied, "Hey, you want to go to America, right? Now you're afraid of a boy from Shiraz?"

He was unaware that this boy from Shiraz would change my destiny. Borhan was twenty-two years old, and I was twenty. My father said, "Marry this boy; I will also cover his cost of travel so that both of you can go to America. Why would you want to go alone?" I fell silent; my grandmother said that silence is a sign of compliance. I said, "yes," and we became fellow-travelers for forty-five years.

Borhan always encouraged me to continue my education. I went to Shiraz and took a teacher training course. We went to Tehran, and I got hired. I also took a graduate class on teaching high school and became the number one student out of 400 students. When Borhan saw that I was always the top student, he said, "What are you waiting for? Go ahead and get your master's degree." After my master's, I completed one year in a doctoral program, however my motherly duties did not allow me to finish the doctoral program.

I spent many years in teaching and educational affairs. I remember when a letter was sent to schools in Iran that asked students to write about the twelve articles of the 1963 Iranian reforms, also known as the White Revolution. The school principal asked me to be in charge of this task. I collected the necessary documents, and with the help of the students, we got it ready and named the handwritten book, *A New Resurrection in the Ancient Aryan Land*. The book became number one in Iran, and, on the 16th of the month of Mehr, was accepted by Mohammad Reza Shah in the stadium where we were given a 5,000 toman prize.

You know, I grew up in an Iran where there was no running water, no electricity, no urban development: a time when skin disease and malaria and thousands of other diseases threatened people's lives. Actually, I witnessed the undeniable progress in Iran. The source of my research was in the archives of the heart.

> *What comes from the heart, goes to the heart*
> *Words will find a way in and stay there contentedly*
> *Lucky are those who find themselves in that space*
> *The ones who see with their heart as well*

I worked for many years as an educational inspector. Very soon, I became the boss of the district inspectors. I had forty inspectors working under me who reported to me. This was one of the highlights of my work experiences. Many people assumed that, because I was young, I wouldn't see the corruption and that I wouldn't want to report on the unpleasant assignments. But I uncovered many cases of corruption. I prevented much theft and sabotage—each case has its own story. I became famous for my strictness. My work, language, work ethic, spirit, perseverance, and my conscience pushed me forward in my work. Until one day I received a decree appointing me to the Ministry of Science in the position of vice president. I remember I went to the office of the minister and jokingly said, "I opened the Qur'an and the result was bad. I do not accept this position." He looked very shocked; I said to him, "Actually, I made a mistake about my previous position as well; it doesn't suit me. I am a good teacher."

I returned to my favorite job, and, from that day forward introduced myself to everyone as an advocate, friend, and teacher of all children. That is, until the revolution broke out.

> *There came a man who called himself the spirit of God*
> *Oh you beloved, sacrifice yourself*
> *So that tulips can grow on your graves*
> *And the coffins will no longer need to be cleansed*

One year after the revolution, Borhan went to Paris, began political activism, and stayed there. For a short while, I too went with my younger son, Arash, to visit. But I could not stay there. I wanted to return to Iran. There was an Iranian woman among our neighbors who said, "You are such a simple woman—leaving your husband in Paris to go to Iran in the midst of war and bombings? Why not go to America instead? I usually charge people $5,000 to get them visas for America. But in your case, I suggest, you go to the embassy. If they don't give you a visa, I will get you one free of charge."

I went with confidence to the embassy and easily got a visa for America. I went to Bakersfield with my son and stayed with Mr. Borhan's brother for one year. But, since Borhan couldn't get a visa and join us, we returned to Paris and stayed there for one or two months. I saw that Mr. Barhan, like many of his friends, made it his work to sit on a bench on the Avenue des Champs-Élyseés and draw out plans to save Iran. I realized that Paris wasn't the place for me. I returned to Iran with my son, but:

> *This is not my town, I have no friends here*
> *Expelled from my own town, no one to understand me there*

I returned to Tehran where I became a teacher in a high school with 2,500 students. They said: "We are aware that you know Arabic, so you must pay your obligatory charity, by teaching Arabic for twelve hours a week to twenty-eight students." So I did, and ten of my students passed the university entrance exams. They sent me an appreciation letter in a *khatam* -inlaid frame and requested that I give a lecture to the school on Teacher's Day. I wore my fanciest clothes. Without a headscarf, I went up to the microphone and recited Ferdowsi's epic poem,

> *In the name of God who bestows life and wisdom*
> *Exalted beyond all that thought can encompass*
> *The God of names and places*
> *The God that provides and guides*

The students started clapping and cheering; they thought another revolution was breaking out. The other teachers thought I was going to be crucified and that my time there was over. The principal frowned and didn't say anything. They gave me my award, and I went home.

As soon as I set foot in the school the next morning, the janitor loudly shouted, "The outcast has arrived. Ms. Nayeri, go to the office." So, I went. From the office, they sent me to the main administration. There was a man sitting there wearing slippers, his shirt was un-tucked, and he had a rosary in hand. Only half looking at me, he said:

"There's been a complaint about you that you've behaved thuggishly. Why don't you follow orders and wear a headscarf, like the other fashionable forty million people?"

In response I recited Molana's poem:

> *We look inside ourselves to our present moment*
> *Not the external world and the rumpus*

He replied, "Leave your worthless talk. For now, you take your orders from this committee."

As soon as he said this, I started shouting,

"What else do you want from me? It is my fault for leaving my husband and a university post in Paris to come teach your children Arabic? If you put me in prison, you add another mouth to feed. You better kill me. Do you want my salary? Go ahead, take it. I know how to recite the graveside prayer *YaSeen* . I'll go sit in a cemetery. If I recite that prayer even five times a day for people, I will make more money than I make here with your damn salary."

> *My heart exploded, that was the last straw*
> *I said whatever I wanted to say at that point*
> *I knew that my job was over*
> *I know I had to sit in a corner at home*

I came home and the telephone rang. I picked up the receiver. It was the same man. With a polite tone he said,

"Dear sister Nayeri, I am the man from before. I did not have the pleasure of meeting with you until today. Wouldn't it be a pity if your hands shook, or if your forehead crinkled? I studied your file and saw that you have many recommendation letters. You are a good and respectable teacher. I wanted to say that, in the absence of your husband in Paris, I am at your service. Let me know if there is anything you need. In the meantime, you can rest. Your salary will be deposited into your account each month. Please come over on the first of September. I'll give you a light six-hour job to do in my own office!"

The receiver fell from my hands. I eventually got myself over to my neighbor's door. I said, "Mehri, open the door. This country is gone; there's no place for us anymore." She said, "What happened?"

I replied, "They've got me for misbehaving and now that the interrogator knows that my husband is in Paris, he wants me to go back and work for him in his office. This place isn't for me anymore."

I still had the visa for Paris. My older son was over eighteen. He couldn't leave Iran. I went to Paris with my younger son, Arash, who was no more than eight or nine.

> *Goodbye happy days, goodbye my homeland, Tell me where the good days went,*
> *perhaps they can be found in stories or maybe they are gone forever*
> *As if no one is alive here, there is lots of crying, no time for laughter.*
>
> —Ardalan Sarfaraz[2]

After about one or two months of living in Paris, I saw that Mr. Borhan was hardly busy fighting! At the suggestion of his brother, my son, Arash, and I went to the American Embassy to try to obtain a visa. Many people were rejected in front of us until it was our turn.

The consular asked, "Why do you want to go to America?"

I replied, "I already have a life in Iran. My husband lives in Paris. We have been invited to my nephew's birthday party in America, and we want to go."

The consular spoke Farsi and asked my son, "You want to go to the birthday party?"

Arash replied, "Yes."

The consular believed Arash and gave us American visas. Arash and I entered American in 1986. Six months later, the same woman from Paris got my husband an American visa for $5,000, and he was able to join us.

> *Both of my hands were praying*
> *Whatever God wanted to happen, happened*
> *This is our destiny*
> *Our home was separated from our homeland*

Borhan's dear brother and his wife were very welcoming and really took care of us. Borhan's brother would buy me books and encouraged me to study them. I spent about five or six months studying. In this span of time, I made a book for my son, Arash. I had him start writing the entire alphabet in Farsi in a notebook. I cut out pictures from magazines and glued them inside. It became a study book, he still has it.

> *A as in Ability*
> *B as in Buried*
> *P like Perturbation*
> *C as in out Cold*

One day, Dr. Torshizi called and said Dr. Rahnama was founding and directing a cultural center and was looking for a teacher.

He said, "Are you ready to go?"

I said, "Yes, of course . . ."

I didn't have a car. I had to take four different buses until I got to Azusa. Once I got there, Mrs. Rahnama came and picked me up in her car and took me to the school where there were sixty Iranian students and about two or three Americans. When I was finished teaching, I would sleep there and take those four buses again the next morning to get back home. I taught there for three complete years. In the first few months that I was there, Dr. Shadab from Orange County got in touch with me and requested that I teach my class there, too.

I said, "I don't have a car."

He said, "I will pick you up and drop you off myself."

I started teaching at their cultural center as well, that had almost fifty students. In Los Angeles, Mr. Lajevardi asked me to teach at a cultural center there as well. And I also signed a contract for a local place in the Valley for $250 a month. I taught a class there as well.

Meanwhile, Mr. Haghighi, who worked in radio and whose child was among my students, approached me and said, "Mrs. Nayeri, no one has ever made my child be able to sit still. You were able to make my child sit still and you taught my child as well. Come on the radio, and we can record a session. I said, "I can't go on the radio, but whatever I teach in class can be broadcast." I recorded all of the conversations in class: even the one where I was telling Sasha to come out from under the table. (Sasha was a very naughty child). The classes were recorded five days a week and broadcast for an hour-a-day on Iranian radio. After that, at the suggestion of Mr. Shadjareh, we created a television show called *Zang-e Madrese* (The School Bell). It was really the crew that filmed the classes and broadcast them on television. This yielded many successful Iranian students. Wherever I go, my students come find me.

> *From each class, I have a thousand memories*
> *I love my students, I have patience for them*
> *I'm in love with my mother-tongue and culture*
> *I'll bring my lessons and books at the drop of a hat*

Friends helped me and Mr. Borhan to open a cultural center in Los Angeles called *The Research and Training Center* . We brought Mr. Borhan's books that were shipped from France, and it became the first cultural center where people could come to read. But the biggest thing that I did was to publish a textbook I wrote on Farsi lessons. It was republished five times. Many universities have used it as a textbook. It has been translated into German as well. I, myself, have used it to teach Farsi to 5,000 students. Along with that book, I also created an accompanying practice manual. A student in Iran who studies thirty hours a week and reaches the next level in nine months, can study my book for one hour a week and reach the next level. I've recently written another book, *Farsi Made Easy* , that is a Farsi lesson book for those who do not have access to the training centers. Young people make great use of this book.[3] I also published several poetry collections.

Overall, I am satisfied with my migration. After all this, had I stayed in Iran, I would have died of grief. I had a life for myself there, but here I had to coax the graciousness out of people to please send their children to class so I could teach them Farsi. It had an effect on me. But I told myself, "Sorour, you are here to help people. You are familiarizing Iranian children with their own culture. Your work is sacred. Don't be upset if you came from a high position and are now teaching children at a first grade level."

> *Sometimes, I get really down*
> *A single "no," makes me tired of life*
> *I aged telling myself, Sorour, don't be sad*

Here, I introduce myself everywhere as an advocate and teacher of children. Everyone thinks that, back in Iran, I was also a first-grade teacher. It doesn't matter. I learned a great deal of things in this country. I live in a nice place. I have freedom. I socialize with all kinds of people. I don't judge anyone based on their money or their wealth. I get on a plane and say, "This is mine." I go to the best hotels and say, "This is mine." I go to the best houses and say, "This is mine." I go to the jewelry store and say, "All the jewelry belongs to me." The sun belongs to me. I've come to realize that I cherish every moment of life. According to Sohrab Sepehri:

> *Wherever I am, let me be, the sky is mine*
> *The window, the mind, the air, the love, the earth, are all mine*
> *What does it matter if, mushrooms of nostalgia grow from time to time?*
> —Sohrab Sepehri[4]

I am a proud woman. My honor is in my work, my writing, and my thinking.

NOTES

1. Abbas Yamini Sharif, "Man yare mehrabanam" (I am the kind friend), (n.d.), https://ketabak.org/content/%D8%B4%D8%B9%D8%B1-%DA%A9%D8%AA%D8%A7%D8%A8-%D8%AE%D9%88%D8%A8 (accessed October 26, 2019).

2. Ardalan Sarfaraz, "Bright Days" (1992), http://ardalan-sarfaraz.com/page-6.html (accessed October 26, 2019).

3. See Sorour Nayeri's website at: https://www.farsimadeeasy.com/.

4. Sohrab Sepehri, "Sedaye paye ab" (The sound of water's footsteps), (n.d.), http://sher-farsi1.blogfa.com/category/2 (accessed October 26, 2019).

Sixteen

The First Kiss

Vida Ghahremani

("Honoring the Life of Vida Ghahremani" was performed live by Ziba Shira-zi at the Skirball Cultural Center in Los Angeles on Sunday, April 24, 2016.[1])

I was the first born in my family and the only girl. I have two younger brothers. Since childhood, I was always interested in song and dance. I was singing my heart out twenty-four hours a day, so much that everyone would say, "That's enough, we're fed-up!"

My dream was to learn how to play violin and to sing opera. I say "opera" because my father brought back a gramophone from Europe with 33 RPM records of artists from his time, the 1920s. A good number of these records had cheerful Italian songs, and we called them "Napoli." Without under-standing what they were saying, I learned all the songs by heart and was always singing. I thought that these songs were opera! Everyone was always saying, "What are these sounds she's making up?!"

My father was educated in Europe and was very open-minded. He was an army officer in an artillery factory in the Saltanatabad neighborhood. We lived in a house with a garden in Saltanatabad, in northern Tehran. There was no school there. My mom was at home, teaching us. When I was six years old, they took me to Amiriyeh, in south Tehran to stay with my grandmother so that I could attend school. I was tested at school and since they noticed I can read and write, they put me in the third grade. I stayed with my grand-mother until I was in sixth grade. I would visit my mother and father in Saltanatabad in the summer time.

Imagine Europe and Tehran. Saltanatabad was like Europe: it had clubs, each night there were events with dancing and music. But in Amiriyeh, we had self-flagellation by mourners in the streets. In any case, I grew up be-tween two very different worlds.

There was a world full of joy
With the fresh air of freedom
Full of dance and the sounds of instruments
That you could sing!
There was a world full of sorrow
Full of grief, full of gripe
Sometimes there would be only remorse
It was always lacking something

The entire time I was at elementary school, my mother and father kept promising me that, once I passed the sixth grade, I could go to conservatory to learn how to play violin and sing opera.

I graduated sixth grade at the top of my class in my district. Like I had time left to sleep?! I would spend all my waking hours singing and dancing and playing percussion on the walls. After I would pass out from exhaustion, I would sleep and, in my dreams, I would be dancing ballet. I remember well the day I went with my mother to the conservatory. Mr. Khadem-Missagh sat at the piano and said: "Young lady, show me how talented you are. I will play a note, and you sing it." I sang the notes, and I said that I also knew how to sing songs. He said: "No, thank you dear, it's not necessary."

He thanked my mother a great deal for bringing me and being there since it was a co-ed school and there were fewer people at the time that encouraged their daughters to dance, sing, or play music. That same day, they showed me my overcoat, books, and music notebooks for my mother to buy me so that I could go to school starting on the first day of fall. You can only imagine what joyous feeling I had while waiting for the first day of fall.

The whole day, my heart was happy
I was singing, I was laughing
I was in my own world
I was twirling
I was dancing
In dreams and while awake
I heard instruments
I, atop the stage
could see the audience

At six in the morning on the first day of school, my mother and I got on the bus from Saltanatabad to come to Tehran. Along the way I noticed that we were on a different route than we took the other day when we went to see Mr. Khadem-Missagh at the Conservatory. At the Mokhber Aldole bus stop my mother said we should get off. I told my mother: "But this is not the conservatory!" My mother said: "Your grandmother consulted the Qur'an and said it is a bad omen for you to go to conservatory. We are going to another high school!" If you only knew how hard I cried and bawled my eyes out, asking: "Prey, tell, what is there in the Quran about conservatory that states whether I should go there or not?"

They enrolled me in Shahdokht High School on Shahabad Street. Out of spite, I decided not to study in order to fail so that my mother and father would realize that I was not meant for this school, but whatever I did, I could not fail. I disliked English, though, and it was the only class I had to retake.

> *With one omen my life turned*
> *Joy left me and my smiles dried up*
> *With one omen, happiness left*
> *My heart suffered from empty promises*

A few years passed. One night my mother and I went to the rooftop summer Cinema, Diana. Under the canopy of stars, they played an Iranian film called *Dokhtari az Shiraz* (Girl from Shiraz), starring Farrah Afeatpour who studied at the same conservatory that I had my heart set on going to. She was also getting invited to go to Belgium and Germany to sing opera.

In the middle of the film, they turned on the lights and started selling sandwiches and nuts and pistachios and drinks. Then they announced that *Studio Diana* was looking for a new face for their next film, that of a young girl.

I asked my mother: "can I go?"

My mother said: "Ask your father tonight; if he agrees, then go."

That night I came home and asked my father.

My father said: "All right, go ahead."

It was that easy! Luckily, my grandmother was not reachable in order to consult the Qur'an.

The next day, I went with my father to *Studio Diana*. It was a four-story building. We went up the stairs to the fourth floor, opened the door to the room, and said hello. Four men were seated and turned to look at us quizzically, shocked that a military man would bring his daughter saying: "My daughter wants to be an actress in your movie." The only face that I could recognize was Naser Malek Motiei[2] because, at the time, he had acted in a couple of films that had made waves, and his picture was nestled clandestinely between the pages of the books of all the girls at school. After a few moments had passed, all four of them got up and introduced themselves to us. That very day, they signed a contract with me for 2,000 tomaan to act in their film, *Chahar Rahe Havades* (The Crossroad of Events, 1955). My father's salary at the time was 500 tomaan.

> *Another chance for the laughter on my lips to return*
> *Another chance for the sorrow to leave and happiness to return*
> *Another chance to sing and dance again*
> *Another chance to fly*

The director of the film was Samuel Khachikian.[3] His films differed from other films of the day. The first scene of the film was of Malek Motiei and me sleeping on the ground. My head was on Malek Motiei's shoulders and his head was on my shoulders; we would crack jokes and laugh together. Khachikian was very European in his movie-making style: he also shot a kissing scene of us. Malek Motiei was going through his military training duty. When the film was ready and they wanted to screen it, the army threw a party for the premier in *Cinema Diana*. The entire military was there. My father and I went as well. The entire time, my stomach was in knots wondering where in the film that kiss would be—until the happy ending: a lip-to-lip kiss. In fact, the last shot stayed on our kiss and froze. After the ending, the credits rolled over the freeze frame of our kiss a whole five minutes. No one made a single move! There were staring at the cinema screen. I was terrified, discreetly glanced at my father and saw that he was looking at me adoringly. With pride he told me: "You finally broke that taboo!"

My mother also didn't have any qualms about my acting in films; she was even happy about it and was proud of me. However, a good amount of family shunned us after that film and didn't socialize with us anymore. My high school also dismissed me, claiming that I was a source of moral corruption. They didn't even let me take my final exams. My mother tried everything she could, to get the school to give me permission to take my exams so that I could get my diploma; but they didn't allow me.

> *I travelled through both the good and bad*
> *past days that never returned*
> *Bitter or sweet, whatever is was*
> *It passed like the wind, and never returned*

Let me tell you that in my work environment and film-making in general, they looked after me. They kept me sheltered, lest someone should say something disparaging to me. I, myself, was very comfortable in that environment, but I was in love with a young man that I had known since childhood, and he didn't like that I acted in films. He was so opposed to my acting, that he attempted suicide and was taken to the hospital. He would say: "Choose either me or film."

I said: "To hell with film; I love you. What do I need film for?" We got married.

> *My best day, is seeing you*
> *My best words, are talking about you*
> *Life, being and existence*
> *is nothing but wanting, wanting you*
> *My best memory, is of you*
> *the keepsake of my life, is you*
> *The longest journey for me*
> *the smallest distance away from you*

David, my husband, and I really wanted to build a place for youth, a place where young artists could showcase their talents that would become a gathering place for young people and people who appreciated the arts. We opened Club Cucchini. [4] We bought the basement of a building and started decorating it. I painted burlap and put it on the doors and walls. It turned into a unique place. It really blossomed within the young community; a lot of the young singers of the time started their careers there and achieved fame.

Per my husband's request, I didn't act in any films for quite some time. Once again Samuel Khachikian pleaded with for another film called, *Toofan dar Shahre Ma* (Storm in Our Town), [5] and strongly urged me to act in it. I said: "Don't even talk to me; I don't have the patience for shouting and fighting with my husband at all." He pleaded so strongly with my husband that he finally came around. I loved the performing arts, so, I returned.

The entire time I worked on this film, either David (my husband) or one of my brothers were with me. Even so, in the night, at home, we had arguments. "Why did you laugh with such and such? Why did you look at such and such?" We always had these kinds of arguments. We did love each other, but we also hurt each other as well.

> *With one glance our love started*
> *My essence became like lovely flowers*
> *A hundred thousand break-ups and make-ups*
> *Lips were ready to be kissed*

I separated from David for a few years and lived to England alone. While I was there, I studied directing for children's television. I also worked at the BBC for a bit. I returned to Iran and tried once again to rescue our life together, but it didn't work out. We lived together a total of fifteen years, and in the end, we divorced each other. And after that, neither he nor I remarried. Our marriage resulted in a boy and two girls whose very beings strengthened the ties of our relationship. Now, when I think about it, I see that neither he nor I knew how to truly live. If I wanted to tell the entire story, it would become, a multivolume epic.

> *Thousands and thousands of pages*
> *thousands and thousands of memories*
> *Lest there be a day where they escape my memory*
> *At times bitter, but at times sweet*
> *My heart says that the old days were better*

For five years, I acted in films. I costarred with Iranian superstars including Naser Malek Motiei, Fardin, Behrooz Vossoughi, Garsha, and Motevaselani, and many others, until one day my son came home and told me, "Mother, why do they tell me at school that my father's name is Fardin?" I saw that as far as my parents and I were concerned, it wasn't important. But when they started saying idiotic things to brainwash my son, I said: Enough with the films, and I stopped acting. Not to mention that my fame had become a nuisance, when anyone needed money they came after me. People thought I was a millionaire, but stingy! Even directors would tell me: "Come act, and we will pay you after the film is sold!!" And that was that. For a long while, I didn't act in any film.

When my son wanted to take his final exams in high school, my mother said: "You too should go back and get your GED, no one is going to stop you this time around!" I thought, what a good idea. I went and took the exam and passed. Soon after that exam, I took a university entrance examination and got accepted into two programs: medicine in Isfahan and early childhood education in Tehran. I stayed in Tehran and earned my bachelor's degree in early child education. I really wanted to continue my studies. With another student at the university who was a young woman, we sent our transcripts to a few universities in America to apply for a master's degree, but, well, this was during the hullaballoo of the early stages of the [1979] revolution, and the deadline for some had passed.

People would go to Takhte Jamshid Street, lay out their bedspreads, and sleep behind Ferdowsi High School: the U.S. embassy office was located there, and they accepted no more than fifty case files each day. I remember well it was the month of Ramadan. People were sleeping in the streets.

I thought, "Who could obtain a visa in this mess?" So, I went to the North to the house of one of my family members. Two or three days later, my friend from Tehran got in touch with me and said: "My cousin and I were third in line, and when it was our turn, we gave your file as well. Hurry up and come for your interview!"

I immediately returned to Tehran. I had one acceptance letter from Norman University, in Oklahoma, that the deadline hadn't passed. I took it and presented it. They gave me a four-year visa. I mean, it was that easy.

> *When it is meant to be, it easily happens*
> *It's not in our hands, whatever will be will be*
> *It's as if in my destiny, it is all written*
> *Good days, bad days, weaving my warp and woof*

The kids studied in Boston and lived with their aunt. I came to America alone in the beginning of 1979 to a town in Oklahoma to attend university. Ten days later, the U.S. embassy hostage crisis occurred. We were four women that lived together, at night, they would throw stones at our home; they really harassed us. I did not last; I went to Los Angeles to be with my mother and brother. For a while, I suffered from severe depression from the horrifying things on the news about all the killings of the Iranian people.

> *Very quickly my dreams dissolved*
> *My delights dissipated and fizzled away*
> *From being saddened of the world*

My heart sank and my eyes were sleepless

Little by little, I found ways to occupy myself. For a while, I was a kindergarten teacher. In 1981–1982, in Los Angeles, I acted in Iranian director, Pari Saberi's[6] play about the life of Forough Farrokhzad, the famous Iranian poet. It was a collage of Forough's poems, combined with poems from Hafez and Rumi. After that, theater became my love, because of the radiating energy of the live audiences and the close relationship between actors and audiences. It was a great experience. I mean, anything that you do is an experience, and there's something to learn from it. And I was in love with learning.

> *A pleasant feeling from gazing into your eyes*
> *From hearing your laugh*
> *Seeing the tears from times of sorrow*
> *That gently roll down your cheeks*

In the early 1990s I performed in *A Night of Love*, a play by Masud Assadolahi.[7] We had lots of performances in America and in Canada. It was a memorable period, even though it wasn't without torment. Producers would take advantage of us financially. Things would not get done on time. We had a lot of difficulties in dealing with venues and stages.

> *We never had it all together*
> *We planted thousands of seeds, but never harvested*
> *If we had a stage, there were no audiences*
> *When we had audiences, there was no stage*

I was in San Francisco with my daughter, Torange in 2005–2006, when a woman called and said: "My name is Mariam. Are you familiar with Vayne Vang?!"

I said: "Who?"

She said: *Vayne Vang*, the film director. Can I give him your number?

I didn't know who he was, but eventually, I told her: Sure, you can give my phone number to whomever you wish.

Now what was up with that Ms. Mariam?

Ms. Mariam had a print shop that film director Wayne Wang[8] occasionally used to copy his works. That day, in my good fortune, Wayne Wang's personal copier broke, and he went to Ms. Mariam's place. While he was copying out his scene, he told Ms. Mariam: I'm looking for an old, Iranian lady who speaks a little English. Ms. Mariam had seen my performances at Golden Thread,[9] my daughter Torange's theater company.

Very quickly, someone from New York called and said: "Wayne Wang wants to make the film 'A Thousand Years of Good Prayers.' I'll send you the scenes now, and I've highlighted a section of it. Please perform that part in front of a camera and send it to us via overnight mail." My daughter, Torange, came with a handheld camera and filmed me. We sent it. The next day, a man called and said: "Wayne Wang saw the clips that you sent and liked it. He wants to have lunch with you." We made plans and Wayne Wang came. He didn't drive himself, his young wife who was a famous actress in Hong Kong came to drop him off. She greeted us and told me: "You are the Meryl Streep of Iran, and you really look like her as well, " and she left, and we sat together. It was as if we had known each other for fifty years. We spoke to each other with ease, we talked and we laughed; immediately after, he sent me a ticket to fly to Los Angeles, to meet the male actor, Henry O, playing opposite me. Two weeks later, we went to Spokane, Washington.

The experience of working with them was very different from my previous experiences with Iranians. I also played in the film *The Rock* with Sean Connery as well (Although they cut that scene in the final edit), but, honestly, it isn't important to me at all, what's important is that I was there and saw all the happenings. Even stranger for me was that the young director of the film was wearing jeans with rips in them, walking around, and telling Sean Connery, a cinema legend, what to do!

Just recently, I starred in a film with Maz Jobrani. That was also a good experience. That group was all American as well. The last play that I was in was with my daughter Torange's theatre company, and it was called "Isfahan Blues."[10] We worked on it for two years. It's about the journey of Duke Ellington to the Middle East.

My daughter was very enjoyable to work with, and I learned a lot from her. My other daughter is a painter; she teaches at a university. My son has combined the arts and computers and is artistic in his work, and he has his own business.

In these days of the diaspora, I've made a series of greeting cards. I've painted the designs myself. You know, I didn't know how to do a business with them; I was left with the lot of them. I wrote and published a couple of autobiographical books: *Safar e Khaash Mahe Asal* (Honey Moon Trip to Khaash) and *Aroussi e Khaleh va . . .* (Auntie's Wedding and . . .).

To be honest with you, I'm not at all happy with my migration. I don't consider the time I've spent here to truly be a part of my life. I love every speck of earth in Iran. Though I don't own anything there. I mean, I was never after buying a house or buying land or buying this and that. But it feels like all of Iran is mine.

> *This home is lovely, but it is not my home*
> *This home is so beautiful, but it is not on my homeland's soil*
> *This city is vast, but it is a strange city, as no place I go is my home*
> —Khosro Farshidvard (in Persian)[11]

But it feels like all of Iran is mine!

NOTES

1. See YouTube video of the full performance honoring Vida Ghahremani's life at Ziba Shirazi, "Life Of Vida Ghahremani," YouTube video, 53:30, posted by Ziba Shirazi & Friends, June 19, 2018, https://www.youtube.com/watch?v=7a-jsWkKSaY&list=PLIENgM7GUZ1w SmEfZK1gjPKJ9ps1LBrtg&index=16&t=6s (accessed September 30, 2019).

2. Naser Malek Motiei was an Iranian actor who played in numerous films. See Wikipedia, s.v. "Naser Malek- Motiei," last modified September 24, 2018, 14:42, https://en.wikipedia.org/ wiki/Naser_Malek_Motiei (accessed September 30, 2019).

3. Samuel Khachikian was an influential film director in Iranian cinema. See Wikipedia, s.v. "Samuel Khachikian," last modified July 24, 2019, 00:13, https://en.wikipedia.org/wiki/ Samuel_Khachikian (accessed September 30, 2019).

4. Club Cucchini a historic 1960s performance space. See Wikipedia, s.v. "A Small Café" (Persian), last modified March 2, 2018, https://fa.wikipedia.org/wiki/%DA%A9%D8%A7 %D9%81%D9%87_%DA%A9%D9%88%DA%86%DB%8C%D9%86%DB%8C (September 30, 2019).

5. CICinema, *Toofan dar Shahre Ma* (Storm in Our Town), *CIC*, 2018, https://cicinema.com/en/movies/6657/storm-in-our-town-1958 (accessed October 4, 2019).

6. On Pari Saberi, see Wikipedia, s.v. "Pari Saberi," last modified February 18, 2019, 23:46, https://en.wikipedia.org/wiki/Pari_Saberi (accessed September 30, 2019).

7. On Masud Assadolahi, see IMDB, "Masud Asadollahi," *IMDb*, https://www.imdb.com/ name/nm1180698/ (accessed date September 30, 2019).

8. See Wayne Wang's A Thousand Years of Good Prayers (2007) at Wikipedia. s.v. "A Thousand Years of Good Prayers," last modified September 12, 2019, 22:48, https:// en.wikipedia.org/wiki/A_Thousand_Years_of_Good_Prayers (accessed September 30, 2019).

9. Golden Thread is the first American theatre company devoted to the middle east. See https://www.goldenthread.org/ (accessed October 4, 2019).

10. Isfahan Blues, "About Golden Thread Productions," *Golden Thread*, https://golden-thread.org/about/ (accessed September 30, 2019).

11. Khosro Farshidvand, "Khaneh" (Home), (n.d.), https://shahrvand.com/archives/92514 (accessed October 26, 2019).

Seventeen

The Doorbell Ring

Zohreh

The sound of the doorbell and telephone ringing bothers me. I always think that something bad has happened; Because when I was thirteen, one night, state security agents barged into our home at two in the morning and took my brother Shahram. I lost my father at the age of ten, Shahram was both a father and brother to me. Our whole life changed from that instant, life became politicized, personal desires didn't matter anymore; every incident that occurred was social and about humanity.

On visitation days, we got to know the families of other political prisoners while waiting at the gate. Our political tendencies were different but there was no friction between us. We were all friends and socialized with one another. I first met my husband's family at the prison gate; Saeed, my husband, shared a cell with my brother. Marriage among the families of political prisoners was quite common.

> One loving gaze
> A few honest words
> Falling in love with a glance
> a lasting glance

Saeed and I were not supportive of the Islamic Revolution. We both opposed the Shah, but we knew that things would get worse under the Islamic government; and this is exactly what happened. The Islamic Republic rooted out the political activists from the very beginning and threw many of them in prison, executed them, and buried them in mass graves. Saeed could not get along with the Islamic Republic, they sabotaged every business he started. He would say, "When I went to prison under the Shah's regime, at least my enemy had some sense, but these people have no culture or sense!"

157

Sometimes I think the regime was happy to see the political activists leave Iran one after another.

The pens turned and they got the upper hand, the tables turned and they took over Iran
Using capricious motivations and excuses, Muslim and non-Muslim were imprisoned
—Hadi Khorsandi[1]

Migration was not an easy decision for me, it was so difficult to let go my mother, but, our son was born, and we neither could nor wanted to live in Iran. First, Saeed went to Austria and got his residency, a year later, my son Omid and I joined him. Europe was nothing like what I had imagined, everything appeared cramped and small to me; even though Saeed tried really hard to get a good apartment, but getting accustomed to that lifestyle was not easy, especially since learning German was difficult for us. Of course, I must admit that we didn't put much effort into learning the language either, my three-year-old boy who just started talking, become our official translator. In Austria, we met some other Iranians, including a rich man who said he is prepared to help us in any way he can to go to Canada, perhaps from there we could get ourselves to America.

Saeed and I went to the Canadian embassy and said, "We want to go to Canada to invest."

The consul asked, "Can you bring a statement from your bank to show that you have $100,000 dollars in your account?"

Saeed firmly said "Yes!" based on the promise his friend had made.

Right there they gave us a Canadian visa and soon we were Toronto bound, oblivious to how with this visa, we have no work permit and cannot receive any government assistance! Back to square one again.

It is hard to build a life anew!
Again, the fear of winning and losing
It is hard to move from one strange land to another
With no chance to build intimacy

We started life in Canada at the bottom. Saeed was working for an Iranian gentleman without a work permit, but we could not make ends meet with that wage. God bless him for letting us live under his shop to at least not have to pay rent. It was an enormously large place. It was impossible to furnish that place with the little basic things we had. I used every ounce of design talent I had to decorate that home, for example . . . I drew fabric over one big cardboard box with absolute precision which became a table and I put a flowerpot on top of it, and it was very pretty.

One night we invited a young married couple for dinner, who had a very naughty kid. The kid jumped around allover and fussed so much that he suddenly fell on my so-called table. The box was crushed and tipped over on one side, as though it was grimacing at us. The poor kid was shocked, taking one look at the table and one look at me! I quickly hugged the kid and said,

"It's ok, auntie, it's no problem at all." Then I explained to the parents that the table was my own handiwork. The kid's mother tried to keep me from feeling embarrassed by saying:

"Wow, how pretty and tasteful . . . extraordinarily innovative. . . . As I walked through the door, I could tell you are one of those Iranian ladies with great taste." And after that they did not socialize with us.

> *Life must be lived, at times with a red rose*
> *At times with a pained heart, at times with a faint glimmer of hope*
> —Sohrab Sepehri[2]

Since my son Omid did not know English, it was hard for him to make friends with other kids. We both felt lonely, both of us yearned for someone to knock at the door. We prayed that someone would come to our home. At last, one day the doorbell rang. My baby, Omid, would scream with happiness and run all over the house, yelling, "Mom, the doorbell is ringing . . . mom the doorbell is ringing . . . someone has come to our home!" Both of us lunged and opened the door. It was Saeed! We were so disappointed. I told Saeed, "Why did you do that?" He said, "Because you both wish so much that someone would ring the doorbell." He was right; hearing the sound of the doorbell had become a dream for us.

> *No matter when you hear the doorbell*
> *Open the door, open the door, God has arrived*
> *You and I know the pain of loneliness*
> *You and I can read each other's eyes*

I remember one day in the elevator at our home, two people were speaking German; Omid started speaking with them and both would reply to him with smiling faces. My baby did not want to come out of the elevator. He was insisting they stay and talk to him. From next day on, he would go to the window and stick his head out and say in German, "Hey people, we don't know English; if you speak German, come talk to us!" I hope the pain of loneliness befalls no one; it's a horrible pain

> *No one should ever feel the loneliness I felt*
> *No one should be so overwhelmed in their life journey*
> *Oh God, may no one be left behind by the caravan*
> —F. Moshiri[3]

I had a friend in Austria who had a naughty daughter named Bahareh. Whenever Bahareh was going to visit our home, Omid would panic, because she would put all his toys under her arms and say these belong to Bahareh! My kid had been so lonely in Canada, that he was even content to be with Bahareh; he would say: "Even if Bahareh comes here I would love her."

> *We have been through many hard days*
> *We had nothing but hope*

Forlorn days without a companion
In pursuit of a bit of kindness

The entire time we were in Canada we looked for a way to reach America. Finally, one day, my brother-in-law with one of his friends, Hassan, who had an American wife, came to help Omid and me cross the border. My husband Saeed, Omid, and I sat waiting in a restaurant on the Canadian side of the border. You can guess how we felt. Hassan pick up Omid and I as though we were his wife and child and we went to cross the border. Oh, what we had to go through! The official at the border look at our passports and wanted to look in the trunk and said, "That's a lot of luggage you've got!" Hasan answered with a laugh, "You know how women think about everything! Especially if they are OCD!" He said, "Fine." and we passed. I was still in shock and I could not believe we were on American soil. My brother-in-law in the United States as just crying when he saw us.

Though exhausted, we made it in the end
It was here that we saw sunny days
I no longer dare to travel
I will no longer take risks

A month later, Saeed went by himself to the American embassy in Canada and got his visa. As soon as he entered America, he applied for asylum; they accepted with ease as signs of torture were still on his body. This was our third migration. First Austria, then Canada, and now the promised land of America. Omid, who was now seven years-old, was delighted to see family and people who spoke the same language, and every day he would say, "Mom, let's stay right here and get adjusted." "For God's sake, let's not go anywhere else." We did just that and once again we started to build a new life.

Our first job was delivering newspapers, we were working three shifts. We worked very hard, and it was not fruitless. Little-by-little, Saeed continued his studies and started working in his own field. I also took a course in drafting and found a job in an engineering office. Life got better and better . . . we all got settled in. Overall, we are satisfied with life in America.

One must live, at times with the simplest tale of a human
At times with a halo from a hidden burning
at times one must laugh at an endless grief
—Sohrab Sepehri[4]

My older son Omid went through tough times. Later when he grew up, he said, "I never found my own identity in school. I didn't know which side I was on. At lunchtime in school, I didn't know whether to sit with the American kids or the Iranians or other nationalities." In the 1990s when there was a lot of racial divisions here, Omid got into a series of problems, but that's a whole other story.

My child asks me where he is from
I say Iran. He asks why he is here
Where there is no green, white, and red flag
on the rooftops

My second son who was born here has a completely different experience. He has four close friends, each one from a different religion and race. He sees no color, no religion, and no nationality. The boys are both happy they are here; they both consider themselves American. They say,

"This country is our home."

"We don't know any place other than here."

"We have no memories of any other country."

Me?? I also consider myself belonging to here. Maybe also because when I went to Iran after many years, I noticed that society no longer accepts me. The conversations with my old friends in Iran always end up in dead ends. Our differences have increased, we do not have much in common anymore.

For my memories not to fade away
I took a trip to that land
A vagabond in search of days of youth
Days that have passed and you only now appreciate them
Slowly I have searched and searched everywhere
How should I say it?
Everything was new, and I was looking for our pasts

You know what it is? I don't know how to live there anymore. It takes a special slyness and cleverness that I do not see in myself. As you get into a taxi, everyone knows you have been far away for years. I don't know if it is because we say hello! Or we say thanks! Or at how gently we close the car door!

When I went to Iran with my younger son, we got into a taxi and paid twice as much as my mom for the same ride. Mom said, "Next time when you sit in the taxi, don't talk so much so they know you are coming from abroad, so they rip you off!" One day with my son, we got into a taxi; the driver said, "Ma'am, I'll turn on the air-conditioning if you are hot!!"

I said, "No thanks, we are fine."

Again, he said, "Do you want the handle to lower the window?" Taxi drivers usually take off the handles so that passengers cannot raise or lower the windows that may break it!

I said, "No sir, thank you though."

A few times I asked my son a question, but he just stared at me and would not answer. When we got out, I said, "Why did you become mute and not say anything??" He said, "Did you not hear that grandma said to not talk or they will charge you a lot?!!" My heart aches from how my own compatriots and those with whom I speak the same language do not consider me as one of them.

As Saeed gets older, he notices more problems of the host society. Sometimes he thinks of returning to Iran. He says, "Over there is our country and, in the end, there are things that can be done," though he is hesitant

> *All this fervor for flight in my head*
> *With the blue sky all around me*
> *Behind the window with my gaze to the heavens*
> *The heart says to go or not to go*

Me? No, I am tired now. It has been twenty-four years since I left. . . . I have had thousands ups and downs, I no longer have the stamina to start anew. I am tired; I am very tired.

> *All this fervor for flight in my head*
> *With the blue sky all around me*
> *Behind the window with my gaze to the heavens*
> *The heart says I'm tired, I cannot go*

NOTES

1. Hadi Khorsandi, "Ghalam charkhid" (The pens turned), (n.d.), http://www.asghar agha.hadikhorsandi.com (accessed October 26, 2019).

2. Sohrab Sepehri, "Zendegi bayad kard" (Life must be lived), (n.d.), http://sherfar-si1.blogfa.com/category/2 (accessed October 26, 2019).

3. F. Moshiri, "Tanha" (Alone), (n.d.), http://sherfarsi1.blogfa.com/category/19 (accessed October 26, 2019).

4. Sepehri, "Zendegi bayad kard."

In Place of A Conclusion

A Selective Analysis of the Themes of Iranian Diaspora

Along with migration comes the pain of separation, fear of the unknown, and hardship that one hopes might lead to adjustment, acculturation, and growth. As one migrates, one combines the homeland's culture, language, rituals and practices, and values and norms with the culture of the host country through various interactions. It is through these interactions that one decides, consciously or unconsciously, what to keep and what to let go of from the homeland in order to survive in the host country. Throughout this process of psychological acculturation, one learns and adapts to new behaviors that are appropriate for the new cultural context. This, according to John W. Berry, means "unlearning of aspects of one's previous repertoire that are no longer appropriate."[1] Young Yun Kim refers to this process as gaining "host communication competence," meaning gradually gaining the capabilities that are needed to actively engage in the host countries, among them "nonverbal codes, norms, and practices."[2]

William Safran believes that a diaspora community is a "metaphoric designation for several categories of people: expatriates, expellees, political refugees, alien residents, immigrants, and ethnic and racial minorities *tout court.*"[3] Asma Sayed points to the emotional, psychological, and mental state of immigrants that change along the way of moving from one geopolitical space to another. Diasporas, she writes, have "both positive and negative outcomes: cultural hybridization, hyphenated identities, a sense of homelessness and non-belonging, fear of assimilation, economic stability, enrichment of literature and pop culture, and deterritorialized cultures."[4] In the final analysis, we take the above categories by Sayed, Kim, Safran, and Berry, along with Victor Turner's four stages of Social Drama—breach, crisis, redressive performances, and reintegration/schism—to explore the stories that came in earlier chapters and develop categories on the themes of Iranian diaspora.

STAGES OF DIASPORIC JOURNEYS AS SOCIAL DRAMA

First Stage: Pre-migration as *Breach*

The eruption of the Islamic Revolution in 1979 and the subsequent war with Iraq tore the fabric of social life for many Iranians. People faced chaos and a sense of uncertainty in their daily lives. The new ruling ideology of the Government of the Islamic Republic created a feeling of alienation in the country, which many more secularized Iranians compared to a foreign invasion. Soon many Iranians were living simultaneously in two worlds and experiencing a deep duality between their private and public lives. In their private lives, they created an enclosed world that maintained their values and beliefs. But in their parallel public life, they observed a set of public norms enforced by Islamic vigilantes on the streets and at places of work or in schools. Families had to teach their children to behave in this new bifurcated way, that is, to teach them to lie to their teachers and authorities from a young age. Eventually, either because of the violence of the new theocratic regime or the complete dissonance between public and private lives, some decided to leave. Leaving behind family members and loved ones and the pain of separation was not easy to bear. Yet the yearning for freedom and a better life compelled many to leave, sometimes without even taking their belongings with them. Turner has characterized this stage as a stage of breach, a tear in the social fabric. Some of the most prominent themes in the narratives representing the first stage of social drama are the following: chaos at home, misuse of religion, arbitrary laws, a feeling of longing and nostalgia, and a feeling alienated. Those who had participated in the revolution, as well as others, were now subjected to purge campaigns and feared for their lives. Many experienced living in a dual reality. This stage ended with farewells to family, friends, and the homeland.

In our collection, all of these themes emerge in the stories told by the participants about the first stage of their diasporic journey. Take, for example, the theme of chaos at home as the participants experienced it in the streets or at work. Here are some statements that highlight a sense of breach in social norms: Fariba spoke of "a checkpoint in the neighborhood where they searched our car and everything we carried in our handbag."[5] Valentina spoke about the pervasive fear that many experienced at the time when they were constantly arrested by the Morality Police for socializing with members of the other sex.[6]

Another common theme was feeling homesick at home, feeling alienated. These feelings of alienation and being homesick at home were exemplified in the narration by Fariba: "The second floor of our building became a militia camp. . . . We left after they disconnected our electricity and everything in the freezer spoiled, leaving an unbearable smell in the air for weeks. I couldn't believe what was happening . . . It was as if these people were from another planet. I felt alienated."[7]

Another theme that emerged in several stories of migration was that of individuals who were purged and feared for their lives, either because they were religious minorities (mostly Baha'is and Jews) or affiliated with the previous regime. Shahrzad spoke of fearing for the life of her family members because: "their friends were being imprisoned or executed one after another. . . . We were worried about my father's safety because many of his friends had been assassinated by Islamic agents around the world."[8] Nasrin spoke of awaiting a possible execution of her husband Hassan: "They convicted him of the Islamic verdict of 'corruption on earth'; which is the Sharia law's equivalent of a death sentence."[9]

The next theme that commonly emerges in the stories is that of living in duality, for example we read in Ziba's story: "We were forced to live two separate lives: One hidden in our homes, the other out in public. . . . Our life inside was closer to who we were. We held secret parties, we listened to music, we danced our dances, and we laughed. In time we even became addicted to the thrill of our underground joy. Simultaneously, we created a fake persona out on the street."[10]

The next theme that emerges in this stage of *breach* that characterize narratives of diaspora, is the longing for freedom and the dream of a better life. Again, as Ziba points out: "I yearned for freedom . . . go wherever I wanted, whenever I wanted . . . do whatever I wanted . . . wear whatever my heart desired."[11] Or as Valentina puts it: "It was my dream to walk with him [her husband] hand in hand in the park without Islamic guards harassing us."[12]

The final theme in this stage is that of saying farewell to family, friends, and homeland. Here is one example by Ziba: "We immigrated to the West, in the hopes of a finding a better life, one truer to our nature, despite the unbearable pain of separation from loved ones."[13] Although many of the stories that are gathered here are about those leaving home during the early years of the Iranian Revolution, this never-ending stage of *breach* continued in wave after wave of subsequent migrations.

Second Stage: *Crisis* in Border Crossing

Leaving the homeland and crossing the border involved either the deployment of means of deception or an open and sincere expression of one's intentions to migrate. Some individuals were smuggled out of the country, while others were able to escape by pretending to leave for a vacation or to study abroad. In either case, those who were able to leave faced a challenging new world of language, communication, and cultural barriers, along with a sense of homesickness. In exploring this new world, they often experienced a cultural shock, feared the unknown, experienced a drastic change in their social status, and struggled to find survival jobs. Many of the new immigrants who applied for asylum (based on their political or religious background) were provided with basic social services and some relief for a limited time which helped them to manage a life with the bare minimum. This stage border-crossing involved a *crisis* of identity for many. Participants constantly and relentlessly compared their old social status and cultural norms with the host country's new rules and norms. During this stage, the new immigrants attempted to come to terms with the cultural norms and behaviors of their new host country, in order to repair the order that had been broken by the breach to make sense of the new circumstances. [14]

The following section documents many of the themes that express this second moment of *crisis*, the border crossing. Common themes include having to engage in deception and denial, both at home, in order to leave, and abroad in order to enter. It also involves economic hardship and loss of status while working in survival jobs. Stories often include a feeling of homesickness, alienation (*ghorbat*), separation from a partner, and migration within migration, as the new migrant moves from country to country to find a permeant home. New immigrants often experience both prejudice and pride simultaneously. They are at the receiving end of insulting prejudicial treatments while also experiencing pride in their own survival skills. This is also a period of heightened political and religious activity marked by immigrants seeking asylum, and joining opposition groups in the diaspora. Here we see distinctions between different waves of immigrants and the transformations they experience when crossing the border.

The theme of "deception in border crossing" often begins at home, and continues at the border and abroad. Nasrin's story provides an example of this: "Finally, we made contact with a smuggler who promised to get us a U.S. visa. I was so naïve, [that] without any question I gathered the money he had asked for and handed it to him. He got us a visa for Italy. . . . When we entered Italy, I realized that the visa didn't include the girls!"[15] Migration often involves lying about the reasons for one's entry: A migrant might say I want to come to the U.S. "to sign a contract and go back to Iran," or "to see Disneyland and also a Michael Jackson concert!"

Some paid exorbitant sums for an invitation from abroad. Valentina "paid $3,000 to a family friend to help her procure a visa to enter Holland."[16] Deception may include self-deception and denial as well. Nasrin says: "The next day, with the ultimate naiveté, I went to the address that the smuggler had given us. That address didn't even exist. . . . But I didn't want to believe that. I kept trying to convince myself, maybe if I don't find it today, for sure I will find it tomorrow."[17]

The next theme that emerges in this stage of crossing borders is that of economic hardship marked by loss of status, the need to engage in survival jobs, and the difficulty of taking care of one's family. Again, Nasrin says: "I had no money to eat. If I could get ahold of any food, I would give it to the girls. Sometimes, for a few days, I wouldn't eat anything . . . not even a piece of bread. . . . I had no choice but to move into a train station where the homeless stayed at night. . . . I went early in the afternoon to find a good place . . . somewhere less windy, [to keep my children warm]."[18] In Ziba's story we read: "In the spring of 1985, my sister and I set foot in America with $2,500 without a work permit. . . . We lived day by day. At the end of the month we would set aside money for the next month's rent [and] buy a sack of rice and a few cans of tuna."[19]

The stories from this early period involve recollections of experimenting with multiple jobs and taking multiple roles that often involve a loss of status. Shervin said: "I was Mr. Architect 'til the pager went off, and I became the [limo] driver to go pick up a client. . . . But I was constantly thinking about finding my way back to my own field."[20] Nasrin had to stand at an intersection to sell newspapers, "crying for hours." Haik delivered Chinese food.

The experience of homesickness is common to all immigrants. Iranians in diaspora often refer to this as being in *ghorbat* (living in a strange land), feeling *gharib* (stranger). The Persian term refers to itinerant people in the Middle East who move from place to place and have no home. Valentina describes this feeling during the early period of migration as: "It was a tough time. I felt the pain of alienation in the core of my being."[21] Massy refers to this pain as a trauma: "You see is a support group for those who face trauma in any way, for those whose homes caught on fire, those who lost a loved one, those who face a life-threatening sickness. . . . We have faced a trauma too; we lost our homeland. We have no one to talk with in our language; these gatherings are like a support group for us."[22]

Separation from a partner is another common theme in the stories. Fariba for example left Iran first and waited for her husband, Farrokh, who joined her six months later. For some of the participants, separation from a partner took much longer than expected: Nasrin said: "For almost three years, Hassan and I lived apart from one another. Our refugee status stalled in both Italy and the US."[23]

Another common theme in the stories is that of multiple migration moves—sometimes by force, sometimes by choice. Some had to move from one country to another and from one city to another before they could find a place to call home. Shervin, for example, began his migration inside Iran in childhood from a smaller city to a larger city and then left Iran to pursue a university education in France to advance his career. He returned to Iran after graduation but again had to leave Iran after the revolution. First, he went to Paris, then to Idaho, and finally settled in Los Angeles. Nasrin started her migration from Iran to Turkey, then to Italy, and finally settled in Canada. Valentina started her migration from Holland, then to Germany, and eventually settled in Los Angeles.

Pride and prejudice are themes that run throughout stories of life in diaspora in this stage of social drama. In general, new immigrant populations find themselves the object of ridicule and insult and taste the bitterness of prejudice. Over time, many painful stories become a source of humor and cause for laughter. Shervin relates the following story about a confrontation over a parking space: "The lady backed off, [rolled] down the window, and started saying something in English. I didn't understand what she was saying, but in the middle of her screaming, I heard her saying 'Go back to Iran!' As soon as I heard this, I got so angry and shouted back: 'Me go back to Iran? No, you go back to Iran!' She shook her head and left."[24]

Participants also expressed a heightened sense of cultural sensitivity. Shahla describes her experience of an unintended prejudicial remark in a close relationship. Here we see how words are often loaded with action so that they no longer remain neutral.[25]

> Watching my favorite Persian program, and Moein our famous male singer, was singing: *Delam mikhad beh Esfahan bargardam* . . . (I wish to go back to Isfahan / [To] once again see that beautiful city). I was really enjoying the song until Tim entered the room and tried to imitate the singer shouting, *"Yai! Yai! Yai! Yai!"* I am sure he didn't mean to make fun of my culture or insult or hurt me, but the music sounded strange to him, and he was not at fault. Later on, I could even justify it.[26]

The next theme that appears in these narratives involves stories about being granted religious or political asylum. In order to receive social services, refugees had to prove that their life was in danger as a result of the Islamic Revolution. Nasrin recalls the following: "When the Islamic Republic took over in Iran, my husband, Hassan, and I were among the first to be dismissed from teaching positions as part of the Cultural Revolution [in 1980]. They convicted him [Hassan] of the Islamic crime of 'corruption on earth,' which is the Sharia law's equivalent of a death sentence."[27]

Different countries have different criteria for granting asylum. In the United States, the most common form in the 1980s and 1990s was political asylum. In European countries, religious asylum was more commonly granted. Despite their dire predicament, refugees still maintained a sense of agency by consciously choosing the country they wished to settle in. Though Valentina applied for asylum in both Germany and the United States, she preferred the latter: "We would constantly change the dates and story to prolong the application process. Had Germany accepted our application for asylum, we would have lost the opportunity to come to America."[28] Asylum cases were often aided by claiming that one was involved with opposition groups in the diaspora. Los Angeles was a major center of Iranian life in diaspora and the focal point of activism to restore the old monarchic regime. There was a pervasive sense of futility in that period that can be seen in the following passage by Shervin:

> I started pointless political involvements, and going to Persian parties and gatherings along with my wife. Conversations mostly started with the same stupid question of: "How is your business?" and finished with inconclusive arguments between the people who personally advised and alarmed His Majesty Shah of Iran of an upcoming revolution![29]

It is noteworthy that the earlier wave of Iranian immigrants from the late 1970s saw themselves as very different from the later waves of immigration. In the following passage, Massy aptly details the difference:

> You know . . . Iranian immigrants in those days were different from now. Today's immigrants are mostly educated. They speak English. They are more familiar with the system. They emigrated in the hope of making a better future for themselves and their children. But those days [earlier] immigrants were parents who followed their successful, educated children. Most of them didn't speak English and were not familiar with the system. They were lonely and felt out of place.[30]

Having looked at some of the emerging themes in the second stage of social drama, we move to the next stage and its unique characteristics.

Third Stage: Networking within the Community as *Redressive Performance*

While experiencing difficulty in accepting the new situation and doubts about whether they had made the right decision to emigrate, new immigrants start building networks of support as they connect with the people within the diaspora community to find a job or to socialize. Turner calls this third state, the Redress Stage, the "most reflexive or self-conscious part of the social drama."[31] This is a stage where the diasporic community begins to look at itself as a community and raises questions about the direction in which it wants to go. Jane Jackson has argued that newcomers often become involved in activities with their co-ethnics or co-nationals to organize mass communication outlets. "Through a wide range of mediated communication systems such as radio, television, newspaper, magazine, movie, art, literature, music, and drama, non-natives interact with their host cultural milieu without direct interpersonal involvement."[32]

A sense of shared pain and sympathy brings members of the community together. This is not yet a stage where members can settle in and call the new location home. Turner points out that the redress stage also involves moments of *liminal* space. Many are forced to go through multiple migrations in order to protect their family and to find a safe haven. The following section is based on a close reading and analysis of stories that describe the nuances of this third reflexive and self-conscious stage.

Themes in the third stage often focus on networking within the community as redressive performances. There is a heightened awareness of bilingualism, of linguistic barriers, humorous stories about made-up words, mixed messages in non-verbals, accents, and naming. Stories of networking within the community involve sharing pain and joy. Stories of cultural-shock often revolve around gender roles and expectations. Novel attempts are made to distinguish one's identity: "*I am, but I'm not the stereotype of what you think I am.*" There is the formation of an exile culture.

Overcoming language barriers constitutes a form of redressive performance. The common themes that emerge in the stories in this stage involve communication, made-up words, non-verbals (hand gestures, for example), accents, and names and naming. This is a rich minefield of painful and humorous narratives, like the time when one participant, Shervin, was offered a "blue job!"

> Since I had noticed everything in America has a connection to colors, like *green card* for residency, *pink slip* (title) for car ownership, *yellow page* for telephone book, and it is obvious to everybody that *blue* is the color of royalty and the monarchy. I thought to myself *thank God*, somebody noticed what I should really be doing and is offering me [a *blue job*] a very high-class job![33]

Here is an example of making up words: when a nurse asked Farrokh, a medical patient, "What is your reason for seeing a doctor?" He replied, "I have brown shit!" (*bronchit* in Persian refers to bronchitis).[34]

Nonverbal communication is involved in a great many stories dealing with language barriers, as in the example of Nasrin stranded at an airport: "Using body language, speaking half Persian, half English, I cried, I screamed, I hollered, I begged. Finally, I made them understand that I would not be separated from my daughters . . . NOT EVEN FOR A MOMENT."[35]

Speaking with an accent is another challenge in the theme of communication and language in these narratives. New immigrants are often faced with a form of micro-aggression when their names are consistently pronounced wrong. In the story by Farrokh, he says: "My name is Farrokh. Here, here they call me *Fred*. For a long time, they called me *Frock*! A friend of mine told me to change my name to Fred so that Americans would be able to pronounce my name!"[36] In another story Shahrzad says: "I cried because I was tired of telling and explaining to everybody how to pronounce my name. My name is Shahrzad. . . . No, no, *not* Sha-her-zad. It's Shahr-zad!"[37]

Networking is the form in which diasporic communities begin to emerge. Many of the stories in this study describe how at the early stages of migration, people tend to look for those who speak their own language. Every immigrant starts networking within his or her own community to find staples of everyday life, something as simple as finding spices and home foods, looking for jobs, or finding a place to live. Inviting family members to move to the same city, so they may live near each other, and thereby ease the pain of migration, was another way in which Iranians formed diaspora communities. Shervin says: "Slowly we got used to living in Los Angeles, to the point that we invited my sister-in-law and her husband from Ohio to come and live in this city that [*sic*] in many ways was like Iran, to ease the pain of migration."[38]

Sharing the pain of immigration brought the community closer as they began to network. Nasrin who experienced the pain of homelessness, likens this stage to a critical distancing in Brecht's *alienation effect*: "To repay for all the help that was given to us, I opened my door to refugees and accepted them with open arms. Believe it or not, in the midst of all the difficulties, along with some other Iranians, I brought Bertolt Brecht's, *The Chalk Cross* on stage in order to remind myself of my own identity. It was an interesting experience."[39] Shahrzad also expresses this theme of shared pains. As an official translator in an immigration court, she was deeply saddened by every refugee story that reminded her of her own father's experience as a refugee: "I was saddened to hear stories of Iranian immigrants who had lost everything and were now dependent on one person's decision. A judge once told me: 'You are a true translator; Iranians cry in Farsi and you translate their cries into English.'"[40] This networking theme continues with Massy who helps homesick Iranian mothers gather at a senior community center to create their own Persian club where people got together regularly for poetry readings and sharing articles to read.[41]

The next theme that emerges from these narratives is that of *cultural shock*, especially with regard to gender expectations. Many Iranian women experienced a dramatic change in gender roles as a result of migration and life in diaspora. Some gained a greater sense of equality as they worked outside the home and earned a living. At the beginning of her narrative Ziba says: "I had thought of everything BUT to earn a living! I thought it wouldn't make any difference one way or another. The same dreamboat who was to be my husband in Iran, working from dawn to dusk was destined to find me in America!"[42] Towards the end, after living in America for several years, she talks about a new view of her femininity: "I'm no longer hindered by those

idle dreams. I have erased them from my mind. . . . And you know what? I
rid myself of confusing gender norms. Now I think to myself, 'This is how
life was meant to be.'"[43] In another story Nasrin says:

> In the West, I learned about the equality of men and women. I became familiar
> with women's equal rights in the home, in love, and in all aspects of life.
> Feminist concepts had grown and taken root in me . . . I could see quite clearly
> that Hassan was also feeling lost and felt that he didn't know this woman
> anymore, AND rightly so. For that kind, delicate, soft, and patient woman he
> once knew had been transformed into a woman who now strongly put her foot
> down and called out, "I."[44]

Shahla expresses her experience of gaining a deeper sense of gender equality
in the following passage: "For years, I thought I was doing Tim a favor. I
thought that he was responsible for the two of us, and I was just helping him
for the moment. Living in America with Tim allowed me to taste the real
flavor of equality between men and women. Life is full of surprises!"[45] As a
result of this process, Iranian men in diaspora have also faced a new series of
challenges in renegotiating their gender status and redefining masculinity in
more egalitarian relationships.

As one settles and adjusts to the new culture through various stages of
hardship, issues of identity take more of a center stage. The next theme that
appears in these stories is that of distinguishing one's identity—establishing
whom one is by differentiating oneself from the stereotypical identities as-
signed by the dominant culture. Shervin speaks of how often he communicated his identity as an architect while driving a limousine: "I believed the
limousine customers could be the best clients for my architectural work,
because they have the money and if they only knew what a great architect I
am, there is be a chance to find a job. . . . So, I took advantage of every
situation to tell my clients about myself and my education."[46] Describing an
incident when he mistakenly assumed he was being offered a high-level
position, he said: "To show him who I really am, I proudly replied, 'Oh yes
sir. I am very interested; actually, I have my PhD in architecture and urban
planning!"[47]

Iranians in diaspora who were not supporters of the Islamic Republic, had
to deal with both the pain of separation from the homeland and the constant
barrage of negative news and criticism of their homeland through media and
American acquaintances. Fariba says: "I wish I could have lived somewhere
where I could proudly say this is my country. I wish I didn't have to explain
to everybody that I am from Iran, BUT against the Islamic Republic."[48]
Shahrzad who was born in Iran and lived overseas most of her life, says:
"You know what? That government has nothing do to with me. I have nothing to do with Ahmadinejad or Khamenei. BUT Iran is my country, Iran is
my home."[49]

And yet, faced with this constant attack on one's homeland and culture (and for many, their religion), most attempt to maintain some aspects of their native culture in their new homeland. This determination to maintain a sense of one's culture appears both in exile media and personal relationships, in saving family traditions and habits even with estranged ones and observing Persian social rituals. Shahrzad, in her story demonstrates how she teaches her son that respect for the elderly is an essential part of the Iranian identity: "I am sorry to say that when I told you that you are no different from non-Iranians. I was wrong! You are different. *We* are different. I hope you would never go to someone's home without greeting his or her parents and the elderly. Your grandfather and I are respectable human beings."[50]

In the early stages of migration, Iranian-American popular media in Los Angeles—television, radio, and magazines—redefined and constructed a new sense of identity for Iranians in exiles. Hamid Naficy believes Iranian exilic television shaped many lives. "Reflecting the formlessness of liminality, it first emerges as a hermetically sealed collection of audiovisuals put together with great individual effort by producers and addressed to what was thought to be a homogeneous audience."[51] Shahla recalls: "Following the Persian socializing was Iranian grocery shopping. Persian food, and Persian restaurant-going, AND to top it all off, the one-hour of Persian TV shows on Sunday which I anxiously waited for."[52] The insistence on observing Persian social rituals while embracing the host culture's rituals can be seen in Shahrzad's story. She embraced Christmas for the sake of her children, so as not to make them feel different from others: "I wanted my children not to feel any difference between them[selves] and the non-Iranians. So, I put up a large Christmas tree at home, and we all decorated it together. We had the most elaborate Christmas decorations in the neighborhood."[53] And yet, she is critical of Iranians who embrace Christmas but not Persian new year rituals.: "Sometimes it is upsetting to me to see my Iranian friends raising American flags on top of their roofs, and celebrating every non-Iranian custom, but not embracing Persian traditions, including Nowruz, the Persian New Year."[54] The Iranian exile culture is also maintained through film festivals and organizations that sponsor cultural events. As Shahrzad points out: "I started voluntarily helping with Iranian cultural events. I still do. I sell tickets at Iranian film festivals and help them with translations. I do as much as I can. My involvement with Iranian cultural organizations keeps me lively and energizes me."[55] Practicing one's culture in the host country is a sign that the community is establishing a new home for itself. This takes us to the fourth stage of the diasporic journey.

Fourth stage: Finding a New Home, *Reintegration/Schism*

As time goes by, one experiences adjustment and acculturation. Culture, norms, values, and rituals of the host country gradually become a part of one's daily life; memories of sadness and hardship become a source for humor and satire. In Turner's social drama, the final stage is one of either reintegration or schism. In the case of Iranian diasporic communities, both reintegration and schism occur and coexist. The redressive performances in the previous stage help to create new ways of seeing and relating out of the old conflicts. It is noteworthy that for many Iranian women who were raised to become someone's wife and to be taken care of economically, this forced migration led to discovering unexpected strengths. This compulsory independence came at the cost of losing what are considered to be feminine traits in Iranian women. Although one might feel a sense of loss—whether of lost childhood or youth because of this transformation—the experience also brings a sense of accomplishment, self-acceptance and growth. This is what makes migration worthwhile. This is what allows the diasporic community to both reintegrate into a new community and to create a schism, a break from the old home community—to become a community unto itself, different from the community at home. The following section expresses a number of categories and themes that were drawn from a close reading and analysis of the stories in this study.

The fourth stage revolves around the theme of ultimately settling in the new homeland and feeling at home, a process that involves schism and reintegration. The stories highlight episodes of making adjustments, experiencing acculturation, and celebrating accomplishments. But they also explore the themes of lost youth, lost times, still not belonging, and misplacement. For some it also involves an appreciation for greater opportunities in life, an epiphany and appreciation for the host country. These sentiments were expressed in vignettes below.

Shahla, after living through the challenges of an interethnic relationship, concludes that she had made the right decision in marrying an American man: "I noticed at the age of twenty-two, that I made the right choice without even knowing it! I realized that the relationship between two people has nothing to do with their culture, their religion, language, or the color of their skin. People's relationships only depend on their humanness, their beliefs, and their values."[56] Farrokh expresses happiness in finding a new home in a diverse community: "I appreciate and like the fact that this country is so diverse. I feel like the whole world is within a ten-mile radius of my home. The neighborhood bakery is Korean, the restaurant owner is French, the grocery store is owned by a Mexican."[57] Fariba, who almost lost a child, battled cancer, and financial problems, found success as an insurance agent: "Slowly life got better and I opened my own office as an insurance agent.

Farrokh joined me and we became a team, and we got nominated as the most successful insurance agency in California."[58] In her story, Valentina, who came to the United States in 1990 during a period of financial crisis, says they were "too póor to even notice it!" Now she says: "Over twenty years had passed since we immigrated. As life got better and better, we became more demanding and wanted more than just a simple walk around the park! Nowadays we can afford to live well. Financial crises affect us as well! BUT life is good."[59]

However, there is a recurring theme in the stories, the sense of loss that many feel was the price for their new achievements. Shervin says: "When I look back, I see my life full of unfulfilled dreams . . ., as if everything is unfinished. . . . Perhaps if I had stayed in one place, I would have known a smaller world and had a better ending, whether in Mazandaran's mountains, whether in Saari, whether in Tehran, *or* in Paris."[60] Fariba expresses this sentiment as a double loss, losing a homeland and not belonging to the host country: "Now I feel like an alien wherever I go. When I go to Iran for a visit, I don't understand their slang. Their language has changed a lot! I can't connect with them anymore. After thirty years of living in America, I don't belong to this country, either; nor does this country belong to me."[61] Valentina expresses this sense of loss in this way: "I achieved my simple wish to walk in the parks, hand-in-hand with Haik and to continue my education. The only thing I lost after the Islamic Revolution was my teenage years. It was as if my youth had been lost irretrievably: Wherever I search, I cannot find it.[62]

Many parents express remorse about having put their children through the hardships of immigration. Here is how Nasrin expresses this feeling: "Let me tell you about the girls. It took two or three years for them to rediscover themselves. Sometimes I think . . . we stole their childhood from them with our forced migration, a childhood that could have been filled with comforts and pleasures. My kids didn't really have a childhood. They grew up too fast."[63]

The theme of ridding oneself of illusions over a long period of time was brought up in many of the narratives. Farrokh expresses the changes he experienced in the following passage: "It took me *TEN* years to realize my mistakes. It took me *TEN* years to get rid of my prejudice and to genuinely evaluate myself, my culture, my values, and my beliefs. It took me *TEN* years to realize the positive aspects of living in the Western world."[64] Nasrin also experienced this epiphany over time, not just for her family as the reason she emigrated in the first place, but also for herself: "At first, my happiness was for the girls, BUT now I am happy for myself, too. You know . . . even though it took a long time for me to discover the identity I had lost to my unwanted migration, as a human being, I now have a broader perspective on life and myself."[65]

The last theme common to many of the narratives in this stage is expressing appreciation to the host country. This is a time when stories of sad memories become satire and a source for humor and laughter. Participants express a sense of satisfaction with the outcome of their migration. Farrokh says: "Now, I am happy about my migration. . . . I have made two great choices in my life, the second one was coming to America."[66] As Nasrin points out: "I feel that I have gained opportunities that otherwise I could never have achieved had I not decided to emigrate."[67] Massy says: "I am happy about my migration . . . happy [to be] living in this country. I flew as high as I could and took advantage of every opportunity given to me."[68]

As immigrants, we go through a long and arduous process of separation, transition, and incorporation. In between, we cry, we laugh, but at the end, our perspectives on life will change and we feel blessed for having had the chance to experience a rite of passage.

NOTES

1. John W. Berry, "Acculturation: Living Successfully in Two Cultures," *International Journal of Intercultural Relations* 29, no. 6 (2005): 697-712, https://doi.org/10.1016/j.ij intrel.2005.07.013
2. Young Yun Kim, "Intercultural Personhood: Globalization and a Way of Being." *International Journal of Intercultural Relations* 32, no. 4 (2008): 359-68, http://dx.doi.org/10.1016/j.ijintrel.2008.04.005.
3. William Safran, "Diasporas in Modern Societies: Myths of Homeland and Return," *Diaspora: A Journal of Transnational Studies* 1, no. 1 (1991): 83-99, at 83, https://doi.org/10.1353/dsp.1991.0004.
4. *Writing Diaspora: Transnational Memories, Identities and Cultures*, ed. Asma Sayed, *Writing-Diaspora* (Oxford: Inter-Disciplinary Press, 2014), xviii.
5. Monologue 2, 34.
6. Monologue 9, 93.
7. Monologue 2, 35.
8. Monologue 7, 77.
9. Monologue 5, 57.
10. Monologue 1, 24.
11. Monologue 1, 25.
12. Monologue 9, 93.
13. Monologue 1, 24.
14. For more on this see Elizabeth Bell's discussion of Victor Turner and Social Drama in *Theories of Performance* (Thousand Oaks, CA: SAGE Publications, 2008), 108.
15. Monologue 5, 58.
16. Monologue 9, 94.
17. Monologue 5, 57.
18. Monologue 5, 60, 59.
19. Monologue 1, 25–26.
20. Monologue 8, 88.
21. Monologue 9, 97.
22. Monologue 4, 55.
23. Monologue 5, 62.
24. Monologue 8, 87–88.

25. This communication theme is further developed by Stephen W. Littlejohn and Karen A. Foss, *Theories of Human Communication*, 9th ed. (Belmont, CA: Thomson Wadsworth, 2008), 115.

26. Monologue 6, 68.

27. Monologue 5, 57.

28. Monologue 9, 97.

29. Monologue 8, 87.

30. Monologue 4, 54–55.

31. See Victor Turner *From Ritual to Theatre: The Human Seriousness of Play. (New York, NY: PAJ Publishers, 1999)*, 31.

32. See *The Routledge Handbook of Language and Intercultural Communication*, ed. Jane Jackson (New York: Routledge, 2013), 236.

33. Monologue 8, 89–90.

34. Monologue 3, 43.

35. Monologue 5, 58.

36. Monologue 3, 39.

37. Monologue 7, 83.

38. Monologue 8, 88.

39. Monologue 5, 61–62.

40. Monologue 7, 76.

41. Monologue 4, 55.

42. Monologue 1, 25.

43. Monologue 1, 29.

44. Monologue 5, 62–63.

45. Monologue 6, 69.

46. Monologue 8, 89.

47. Monologue 8, 90.

48. Monologue 2, 37.

49. Monologue 7, 83–84.

50. Monologue 7, 81.

51. See Hamid Naficy, *The Making of Exile Cultures: Iranian Television in Los Angeles* (Minneapolis: University of Minnesota Press, 1993), 124.

52. Monologue 6, 68.

53. Monologue 7, 80.

54. Monologue 7, 79.

55. Monologue 7, 78–79.

56. Monologue 6, 71.

57. Monologue 3, 46.

58. Monologue 2, 36.

59. Monologue 9, 98.

60. Monologue 8, 91.

61. Monologue 2, 37.

62. Monologue 9, 98.

63. Monologue 5, 64.

64. Monologue 3, 35–36.

65. Monologue 5, 64.

66. Monologue 3, 36.

67. Monologue 5, 64.

68. Monologue 4, 56.

Bibliography

Abdi, Shadee, and Bobbi Van Gilder. "Cultural (In)visibility and Identity Dissonance: Queer Iranian-American Women and Their Negotiation of Existence." *Journal of International and Intercultural Communication*. 9, no. 1 (2016): 69–86. https://doi.org/10.1080/175130 57.2016.1120850.

Afary, Janet. "Iranian Revolution [1978–1979]." In *Encyclopædia Britannica*. Encyclopædia Britannica. https://www.britannica.com/event/Iranian-Revolution (accessed September 20, 2017).

———. *The Iranian Constitutional Revolution, 1906–1911: Grassroots Democracy, Social Democracy, and the Origins of Feminism*. New York: Columbia University Press, 1996.

Aminpour, Gh. "Goldan-e Khali." (empyty vase), n.d. http://shereno.com/poet-3340.html (accessed October 26, 2019).

Assi, Qahaar. "Geristim." 1989. http://qahaar-assi.blogfa.com/1386/06 (accessed on October 26, 2019).

Auliffe, Sarah. "Popular Music and the Construction in Iranian Diasporic Contexts." *Context* 35/36 (2010–2011): 59–76. https://cpb-ap-se2.wpmucdn.com/blogs.unimelb.edu.au/dist/6/ 184/files/2016/07/35-36_Auliffe-27hcai8.pdf (accessed October 26, 2019).

Austen, Jane. *Pride and Prejudice*. New York: Modern Library, 1995.

Behbahani, Simin. "Delam gereftehh havaye geryeh." In *Dashte Arjan*. Tehran, Iran: Zavvar Publishing, 1991.

Bell, Elizabeth. *Theories of Performance*. Thousand Oaks, CA: SAGE Publications, 2008.

Berry, John W. "Acculturation: Living Successfully in Two Cultures." *International Journal of Intercultural Relations* 29, no. 6 (2005): 697–712. https://doi.org/10.1016/j.ijintrel.20 05.07.013.

Brecht, Bertolt. *Fear and Misery of the Third Reich* (1938). Translated by John Willett. London: Bloomsbury Methuen Drama, 2009. Reprint. 2015.

Brubaker, Rogers. "The 'Diaspora' Diaspora." *Ethnic and Racial Studies* 28, no. 1 (2006): 1–19. https://doi.org/10.1080/0141987042000289997.

Buller, David B., and Judee K. Burgoon. "Interpersonal Deception Theory." *Communication Theory* 6, no. 3 (1996): 203–42.

Burke, Kenneth. *The Philosophy of Literary Form*. Berkeley: University of California Press, 1974.

CICinema. "Toofan dar Shahre Ma" (Storm in Our Town). *CIC*. 2018. https://cicinema.com/en/ movies/6657/storm-in-our-town-1958 (accessed October 4, 2019).

Conquergood, Dwight. "Of Caravans and Carnivals: Performance Studies in Motion." *TDR* (MIT Press) 39, no. 4 (1995): 137–41. https://www.jstor.org/stable/1146488.

———. "Performance Studies: Interventions and Radical Research." In *The Performance Studies Reader*, 2nd ed., edited by Henry Bial, 369–80. New York: Routledge, 2007.

———. "Performing as a Moral Act: Ethical Dimensions of the Ethnography of Performance." *Literature in Performance* 5, no. 2 (1985): 1–13. https://doi.org/10.1080/10462938509391578.

Dartoumian, Manijeh. "Delam gerefteh." N.d. http://dartoomian.blogfa.com/1388/12/3 (accessed October 26, 2019).

Deyhim, Sussan. *The House is Black*. Vimeo video. 02:25, posted by "CAP UCLA." 2014. https://vimeo.com/109868198.

Elahi, Babak, and Persis M. Karim. "Introduction: Iranian Diaspora." *Comparative Studies of South Asia, Africa and the Middle East* 31, no. 2 (2011): 381–87. https://doi.org/10.1080/00210862.2012.740896.

Elahi Ghomshei, Hossein. "The Rose and the Nightingale: The Role of Poetry in Persian Culture." *SGI Quarterly* 51 (2007): 6–8. https://www.sgi.org/content/files/resources/sgi-quarterly-magazine/0801_51.pdf (accessed May 16, 2015).

Elliot, Andrew J., and Carol Dweck. *Handbook of Competence and Motivation*. New York: Guilford Press, 2007.

Ellis, Carolyn. *Final Negotiations: A Story of Love, Loss, and Chronic Illness*. Philadelphia, PA: Temple University Press, 1995.

Farahani, Fataneh. "Diasporic Masculinities." *Nordic Journal of Migration Research* 2, no. 2 (2012): 159–66. https://doi.org/10.2478/v10202-011-0038-5.

Farshidvard, K. "Salaye eshgh." In *Daftare sher*, item number: 15066. Tehran: Omide Majd, 2002. https://shop.ketab.com/book-detail.aspx?item=15066&title=%D8%B5%D9%84%D8%A7%DB%8C%20%D8%B9%D8%B4%D9%82&author=%D9%81%D8%B1%D8%B4%D9%8A%D8%AF%D9%88%D8%B1%D8%AF%D8%8C%20%D8%AE%D8%B3%D8%B1%D9%88 (accessed October 28, 2019).

Farshidvand, Khosro. "Khaneh." N.d. https://shahrvand.com/archives/92514 (accessed October 26, 2019).

Giguère, Benjamin, Richard N. Lalonde, and Evelina Lou. "Living at the Crossroads of Cultural Worlds: The Experience of Normative Conflicts by Second Generation Immigrant Youth." *Social and Personality Psychology Compass* 4, no. 1 (2010): 14–29. http://dx.doi.org/10.1111/j.1751-9004.2009.00228.x.

Gordafarid. "Gordafarid Presents The Story of Gurdafarid and Suhrab // Performances." Vimeo video. 08:42, posted by "LACMA." May 2, 2018. https://vimeo.com/268865001.

Grammy, Tara, and Tom Arthur Davis. *Mahmoud*. Toronto: Playwrights Canada Press, 2015.

Hafez. "Ghazal 365." N.d. https://ganjoor.net/hafez/ghazal/sh366/ (accessed October 26, 2019).

Haggard, Thomas R., with Tracey C. Green and Leigh Nason. *Understanding Employment Discrimination*. 2nd ed. Newark, NJ: LexisNexis Mathew Bender, 2008.

Hakakian, Roya. *Journey from the Land of No*. New York: Crown, 2004.

Hakimzadeh, Shirin. "Iran: A Vast Diaspora Abroad and Millions of Refugees at Home." *Migration Information Source* 4 (2006). https://www.migrationpolicy.org/article/iran-vast-diaspora-abroad-and-millions-refugees-home (accessed September 30, 2019).

Hakimzadeh, Shirin, and David Dixon. "Spotlight on the Iranian Foreign Born." Migration Policy Institute, 2006, https://www.migrationpolicy.org/article/spotlight-iranian-foreign-born (accessed October 1, 2019).

Hamers, Josiane F., and Michel H. A. Blanc. *Bilinguality and Bilingualism*. 2nd ed. Cambridge: Cambridge University Press, 2000.

Harrison, Frances. "Huge Cost of Iranian Brain Drain." *BBC News* (Middle East). January 08, 2007. http://news.bbc.co.uk/2/hi/middle_east/6240287.stm (accessed September 30, 2019).

Hong, Ye. "A Cultural Approach to Literature for Chinese Students." In *English and Globalization: Perspectives from Hong Kong and Mainland China*, edited by Kwok-kan Tam and Timothy Weiss, 205–18. Hong Kong, China: Chinese University Press, 2004.

Houshyarnejad, Houshiarnejad. *Baghe Alefba*. Los Angeles: Asre Emrooz Publishing, 2007.

IMDB. "Masud Asadollahi." *IMDb*. https://www.imdb.com/name/nm1180698/ (accessed date September 30, 2019).

Isfahan Blues. "About Golden Thread Productions." *Golden Thread.* https://goldenthread.org/about/ (accessed September 30, 2019).

Jackson, Jane, ed. *The Routledge Handbook of Language and Intercultural Communication.* New York: Routledge, 2013.

Karim, Persis M., ed. *Let Me Tell You Where I've Been: New Writing by Women of the Iranian Diaspora.* Fayetteville: University of Arkansas Press, 2006.

Kelley, Ron, and Jonathan Friedlander, eds. *Irangeles: Iranians in Los Angeles.* Berkeley: University of California Press, 1993.

Khorsandi, Hadi. "Bogzar az Ney." May 4, 1998. https://iranian.com/Satire/May98/khorsandi.html?site=archive (accessed October 28, 2019).

———. "Varagh Bargasht." N.d. http://www.asgharagha.hadikhorsandi.com (accessed October 26, 2019).

Kim, Young Yun. "Intercultural Personhood: Globalization and a Way of Being." *International Journal of Intercultural Relations* 32, no. 4 (2008): 359–68. http://dx.doi.org/10.1016/j.ijintrel.2008.04.005.

Littlejohn, Stephen W., and Karen A. Foss. *Theories of Human Communication.* 9th ed. Belmont, CA: Thomson Wadsworth, 2008.

MacArthur Foundation. "Anna Deavere Smith." *MacArthur Foundation.* July 1, 1996. Last updated January 1, 2005. https://www.macfound.org/fellows/544/ (accessed September 30, 2019).

Malek, Amy. "Public Performances of Identity Negotiation in the Iranian Diaspora: The New York Persian Day Parade." *Comparative Studies of South Asia, Africa and the Middle East* 31, no. 2 (2011): 388–410. https://doi.org/10.1215/1089201X-1264316.

McCoy, Kansas Joe. "Why don't you do right." Sung by Peggy Lee. 78 rpm records, A side. New York: Columbia, 1942. https://www.songfacts.com/lyrics/peggy-lee/why-dont-you-do-right (accessed October 26, 2019).

Milani, Mohsen M. "The Iranian Islamic Revolution (1979)." In *Encyclopedia of Political Revolutions,* edited by Jack Goldstone, 248–52. London: Fitzroy Dearborn, 1998. Reprint. New York: Routledge, 2015.

Moaveni, Azadeh. *Lipstick Jihad: A Memoir of Growing Up Iranian in America and American in Iran.* New York: Public Affairs, 2005.

Mobasher, Mohsen Mostafavi. *The Iranian Diaspora: Challenges, Negotiations, and Transformations.* Austin: University of Texas Press, 2018.

Moosavi, Marjan. "Acclimatization: Feminist Iranian Theatre Acclimatizes to Diaspora." *Theatre Times.* June 9, 2018. https://thetheatretimes.com/acclimatization-feminist-iranian-theatre-acclimatizes-diaspora/ (accessed September 30, 2019).

Moshiri, F. "Tanha." N.d. http://sherfarsi1.blogfa.com/category/19 (accessed October 26, 2019).

Motlagh, Amy. "Autobiography and Authority in the Writings of the Iranian Diaspora." *Comparative Studies of South Asia, Africa and the Middle East* 31, no. 2 (2011): 411–24. https://doi.org/10.1215/1089201X-1264325.

Naficy, Hamid. *The Making of Exile Cultures: Iranian Television in Los Angeles.* Minneapolis: University of Minnesota Press, 1993.

Nafisi, Azar. *Reading Lolita in Tehran: A Memoir in Books.* New York: Random House, 2003.

Neshat, Shirin, and Shoja Azari. *Women Without Men.* DVD. Directed by Shirin Neshat and Shoja Azari. New York: IndiePix, 2009.

Neshat, Shirin, Ahmad Diba, and Shirin Neshat. *Looking for Oum Kulthum.* Directed by Shirin Neshat and Shoja Azari. Geneva: Agora Films, 2017.

Noorbakhsh, Zahra. "It's Not This Muslim Comedian's Job to Open Your Mind." *New York Times.* May 6, 2017. https://www.nytimes.com/2017/05/06/opinion/sunday/its-not-this-muslim-comedians-job-to-open-your-mind.html (accessed September 30, 2019).

Oberg, Kalervo. "Cultural Shock: Adjustment to New Cultural Environments." *Curare* 7, no. 2 (1960): 177–82. Reprint. *Curare* 29, no. 2 (2006): 142–46. https://www.academia.edu/17206900/Cultural_Shock_Adjustment_to_new_cultural_environments_-_Kalervo_Oberg (accessed September 30, 2019).

Pickett, Leah. Review of "Jimmy Vestvod: *Amerikan Hero.*" *Chicago Reader.* 2016. https://www.chicagoreader.com/chicago/jimmy-vestvood-amerikan-hero/Film?oid=23603696 (accessed September 30, 2019).

Pollock, Della, ed. *Remembering: Oral History Performance.* New York and Basingstoke, UK: Palgrave Macmillan, 2005.

Radmanesh, Babak. "Chegooneh Zendegi Kardan." N.d. http://lifemahin.blogfa.com/tag/%D8%A8%D9%88%DB%8C-%D8%B2%D9%86%D8%AF%DA%AF%DB%8C (accessed October 26, 2019).

Rahnavard, Zahra. "Gorgha." N.d. https://news.gooya.com/politics/archives/2009/06/089067.php (accessed October 26, 2019).

Salimi, Younes. "Khodahafez, Khodahafez." N.d. http://shereno.com/22000/20232/169062.html (accessed October 26, 2019).

Sarfaraz, Ardalan. "Bright Days." 1992. http://ardalan-sarfaraz.com/page-6.html (accessed October 26, 2019).

Safran, William. "Diasporas in Modern Societies: Myths of Homeland and Return." *Diaspora: A Journal of Transnational Studies* 1, no. 1 (1991): 83–99. https://doi.org/10.1353/dsp.1991.0004.

Satrapi, Marjane. *Persepolis: The Story of a Childhood.* New York: Pantheon, 2003.

Sayed, Asma, ed. *Writing Diaspora: Transnational Memories, Identities and Cultures.* Oxford: Inter-Disciplinary Press, 2014.

Sepand, Masoud. "Mabar goman." N.d. massoudsepand.blogspot.com (no longer available) (accessed October 26, 2019).

Sepehri, Sohrab. "Sedaye paye ab." N.d. http://sherfarsi1.blogfa.com/category/2 (accessed October 26, 2019).

———."Original language." N.d. http://sherfarsi1.blogfa.com/category/2 (accessed October 26, 2019).

Sheybani, Jamshid. "Delam mikhad be Esfahan bargardam," sung by Moein. 1990. https://pikdo.net/p/ostad_moein_saeed/2083625683561855049_6087221823 (accessed October 26, 2019).

Shirazi, Ziba. "Life Of Vida Ghahremani." YouTube video. 53:30. Posted by Ziba Shirazi & Friends. June 19, 2018. https://www.youtube.com/watch?v=7a-jsWkKSaY&list=PLIENgM7GUZ1wSmEfZK1gjPKJ9ps1LBrtg&index=16&t=6s (accessed September 30, 2019).

———. "Zan," *Zananeha* (album). Los Angeles: Shirazi, 1998. https://store.cdbaby.com/cd/zibashirazi10 (accessed October 28, 2019).

Spiegelman, Art. *Maus: A Survivor's Tale.* New York: Pantheon, 1991.

Sullivan, Zohreh T. *Exiled Memories: Stories of Iranian Diaspora.* Philadelphia: Temple University Press, 2001.

Talebi, Shahla. "From the Moon to Television: A Story of the Iranian Revolution of 1979." *International Society for Iranian Studies.* Conference paper 8th Biennial Conference on Iranian Studies, Association for Iranian Studies. May 27–30, 1996, Santa Monica, CA. https://associationforiranianstudies.org/node/163 (accessed September 30, 2019).

Ting-Toomey, Stella. *Communicating Across Cultures.* New York: Guilford Press, 1999.

Tolouei, Shabnam. "*Autumn Dance,* by Shabnam Tolouei." YouTube video. 00:52. Posted by Stanford Iranian Studies Program. July 18, 2017. https://www.youtube.com/watch?v=DgjM5s24zMM.

———. "Iran's First Feminist Qorrat al-Ayn is Brought Back to Life in New Movie." Interview with Katayhoon Halajan. *Kayhan Life.* November 16, 2016. https://kayhanlife.com/culture/film/irans-first-feminist-qorrat-al-ayn-brought-back-life-new-movie/ (accessed September 30, 2019).

Turner, Victor. *Drama, Fields and Metaphors: Symbolic Action in Human Society.* Ithaca, NY: Cornell University Press, 1974/

———. *From Ritual to Theatre: The Human Seriousness of Play.* Baltimore: PAJ Publications, 1982.

———. "Liminality and Communitas." In *The Performance Studies Reader*, 2nd ed., edited by Henry Bial, 89–97. New York: Routledge, 2007.

Ward, Colleen A., Stephen Bochner, and Adrian Furnham. *The Psychology of Culture Shock.* 2nd ed. Philadelphia: Taylor & Francis, 2001.

Weems, Mary E. *Blackeyed: Plays and Monologues.* Boston: Sense Publishers, 2015.

Wikipedia. s.v. "Naser Malek- Motiei." Last modified September 24, 2018, 14:42. https://en.wikipedia.org/wiki/Naser_Malek_Motiei (accessed September 30, 2019).

Wikipedia. s.v. "Samuel Khachikian." Last modified July 24, 2019, 00:13. https://en.wikipedia.org/wiki/Samuel_Khachikian (accessed September 30, 2019).

Wikipedia. s.v. "A Small Café." (Persian). Last modified March 2, 2018. https://fa.wikipedia.org/wiki/%DA%A9%D8%A7%D9%81%D9%87_%DA%A9%D9%88%DA%86%DB%8C%D9%86%DB%8C (September 30, 2019).

Wikipedia. s.v. "Pari Saberi." Last modified February 18, 2019, 23:46. https://en.wikipedia.org/wiki/Pari_Saberi (accessed September 30, 2019).

Wikipedia. s.v. "A Thousand Years of Good Prayers." Last modified September 12, 2019, 22:48. https://en.wikipedia.org/wiki/A_Thousand_Years_of_Good_Prayers (accessed September 30, 2019).

Williams, Raymond. *The Long Revolution.* Ontario: Broadview Press, 1961.

Wolpe, Sholeh. "The Outside." In *Rooftops of Tehran: Poems.* Pasadena, CA: Red Hen Press, 2008.

Yamini Sharif, Abbas. "Man yare mehrabanam." N.d. https://ketabak.org/content/%D8%B4%D8%B9%D8%B1-%DA%A9%D8%AA%D8%A7%D8%A8%D8%AE%D9%88%D8%A8 (accessed October 26, 2019).

Yeghiazarian, Torange. "About Golden Thread Productions." *Golden Thread.* https://www.goldenthread.org/about/ (accessed 2018). https://goldenthread.org/about/ (accessed September 30, 2019).

Yousefi, Nahid. "Harkas be tarighi del e ma mishekanad." N.d. https://ayateghamzeh.ir/Poem/ID/107834/%D9%87%D8%B1-%DA%A9%D8%B3-%D8%A8%D9%87-%D8%B7%D8%B1%DB%8C%D9%82%DB%8C-%D8%AF%D9%84-%D9%85%D8%A7-%D9%85%DB%8C-%D8%B4%DA%A9%D9%86%D8%AF (accessed October 26, 2019).

Zaharna, Rhonda S. "Self-Shock: The Double-Binding Challenge of Identity." *International Journal of Intercultural Relations* 13, no. 4 (1989): 501–25. https://doi.org/10.1016/0147-1767(89)90026-6.

Zeine, Foojan, and Mahnaz Attarha. *Mā* (Persian Edition). Bloomington, IN: XLIBIRS, 2014.

Index

Abdi, Shadee, 7

acculturation: defining, 98n1; Iranian cultural traditions relation to, 79–80, 84n3; psychological, 163; scholars/ scholarship on, 13, 14, 84n3, 163; stages of, 13, 14, 84n3, 163

Afary, Janet, 17n1–17n2

alienation: breach stage, 164; duality relation to, living in, 37, 82–84; experiences of, 69, 70, 97, 154, 161–162, 167, 171, 175; under Islamic Republic, 164, 165

All Atheists Are Muslim (Noorbakhsh), 10

Aminpour, Gh., 55, 107

Aristotle, 13

Armenians, 3, 40, 93, 103

Asre Emrooz (magazine), 113, 115

Assi, Qahaar, 120

Assyrians, 3

asylum, political or religious, 137, 160; applying for, 51, 60, 61, 95–97, 168–169; border crossings under, 166; criteria for, 95, 168–169; in Germany, 95–97, 168–169; social services with, 61; status, about, 166; stories created in applying for, 95–97

Attarha, Mahnaz, 8–9

autobiographical works: by Iranian-American women, 8, 154; Iranian Diaspora Studies use of, 7; radio documentaries and, 11

"Autobiography and Authority in the Writings of the Iranian Diaspora" (Motlagh), 7

Autumn Dance (Tolouei), 10

avant-garde ideology, 8, 117

Axis of Evil Comedy Tour (Jobrani), 10–11

Aznavour, Charles, 86, 91

Baha'i, 3, 6, 104, 165

Bakhtiar (prime minister), 49

Barre, Raymond, 122–123

Behbahani, Simin, 120

Berry, John W., 12, 13, 14, 84n3, 163

Bodley, John, 30n2

border crossings, 15; under asylum, 166; as crisis stage, 165–169; economic hardship with, 167; identity crisis with, 166; for Jews, 133–134; kindness experienced in, 104–105; from Mexico to U.S., 134–137; risk with, 94–95, 133–134, 136–137; smuggling/ smugglers for, 58–59, 62, 136–137, 166, 166–167; social status loss with, 167

breach stage of Social drama, 12, 31n6, 163–165

Brecht, Bertolt, 61, 171

Brosnan, Pierce, 89

Brubaker, Rogers, 9

Burke, Kenneth, 72n4

About the Authors

Ziba Shirazi is a poet, singer, songwriter, and storyteller who left Iran in 1985. As an artist, she is best known for her poignant songs and storytelling through poetry. Shirazi's compositions blend together flavors of Persian melodies with world music and jazz. She is the first Iranian female singer-songwriter to write all her own songs, as well as to produce and promote them in seven albums since 1990. Ziba is referred to as the "voice of women" in the Iranian-American community; her lyrics are colored by passionate feminist tones, love, compassion, and universal human stories. Beginning in 2009, Shirazi created the ongoing project of *Story & Song*, a lyrical storytelling series of performances, set to live music with video projections featuring stories of Iranian immigrant families and their struggles since the Islamic Revolution. In the spring of 2014, Shirazi staged her first musical production, *Spring Love*, at the Los Angeles County Museum of Art (LACMA). Her ongoing projects continue to touch audiences' hearts, crossing cultural gaps with her unique art of storytelling. To know more about her work see: http://www.zibashirazi.com.

Kamran Afary is the author of *Performance and Activism: Grassroots Discourse After the Los Angeles Rebellion of 1992* (Lexington Press, 2009). He is an Assistant Professor of Communication Studies at California State University Los Angeles. He is also a Registered Drama Therapist (RDT) at the Drama Therapy Institute of Los Angeles. He has over twenty years of teaching both on campus and in prison education, and professional experience as a radio journalist and documentary-maker, producing programs focused on labor struggles, immigration, and race relations. Afary has contributed to the writing of this book by shaping the analysis of the performance scripts and theorizing this research into a scholarly project.

www.ingramcontent.com/pod-product-compliance
Lightning Source LLC
Chambersburg PA
CBHW021428110726
47901CB00008B/2337